A MILITARY HISTORY OF
ANCIENT GREECE

A MILITARY HISTORY OF ANCIENT GREECE

An authoritative account of the politics, armies and wars during the golden age of ancient Greece, shown in more than 200 photographs, diagrams, maps and plans

NIGEL RODGERS

southwater

This edition is published by Southwater
an imprint of Anness Publishing Ltd
Blaby Road, Wigston
Leicestershire LE18 4SE
Email: info@anness.com
Web: www.southwater.com; www.annesspublishing.com

Anness Publishing has a new picture agency outlet for
images for publishing, promotions or advertising. Please
visit our website www.practicalpictures.com for more
information.

Publisher: Joanna Lorenz
Editor: Joy Wotton
Designer: Nigel Partridge
Illustrations: Vanessa Card, Anthony Duke,
Peter Bull Art Studio
Production Controller: Don Campaniello
Proofreading Manager: Lindsay Zamponi

ETHICAL TRADING POLICY
Because of our ongoing ecological investment programme,
you, as our customer, can have the pleasure and reassurance
of knowing that a tree is being cultivated on your behalf
to naturally replace the materials used to make the book
you are holding. For further information about this
scheme, go to www.annesspublishing.com/trees

PUBLISHER'S NOTE
Although the information in this book is believed to be
accurate and true at the time of going to press, neither
the authors nor the publisher can accept any legal
responsibility or liability for any errors or omissions that
may be made.

PICTURE ACKNOWLEDGEMENTS
The Ancient Art & Architecture Collection Ltd: 5.3,
6–7, 16tl & br, 17t & b, 18t, 19t, 21t, 22tr, 23t & b,
24tl, 25b, 26t, 27b, 28t & b, 30b, 32b, 33t, 34t, 40t,
42b, 43t & b, 45b, 48t & b, 52–3, 56tl, 57b, 58b, 60t,
63b, 64b, 65b, 68b, 69, 71t, 74b, 76t, 84b, 86t, 89, 92l
& r, 97b, 99t, 100br, 102t, 103b, 104, 105b, 110t, 112b,
122br; /Ronald Sheridan 1, 51b, 55t, 103tr, 111b; /C.M.
Dixon 18b, 74t; /M. Williams 30t; /G.T. Garvey 31t,
44t, 100tl; /Interfoto 5.2, 36–7; /Prisma 98b; /D.R.
Justice 114t

The Art Archive: 121b; /JFB 3, 91b; /Archaeological
Museum Naples/Dagli Orti (A) 5br, 35, 79t; /Dagli Orti
5.1, 8b, 22b, 34b, 39b, 41b, 44b, 46t, 54b, 61b, 73t, 81b,
87b, 99b, 110b, 114b, 116br, 120b, 122tl, 124b; /Dagli
Orti (A) 39t, 76b, 78t, 106–7, 118b; /Archeological
Museum Piraeus/Dagli Orti 5.4, 5.6, 14–15, 62, 66–7,
100; /Musée du Louvre Paris/ Dagli Orti 38b, 40b;
/Acropolis Museum Athens/Dagli Orti 8t, 60b, 75t,
77b, 81t; /Heraklion Museum/Dagli Orti 16tr; /National
Archaeological Museum Athens/ Dagli Orti 19b, 21b,
109t; /Museo di Villa Giulia Rome/Dagli Orti 26b;
/British Museum/Eileen Tweedy 38t, 65t; /Jean Vinchon
Numismatist Paris/Dagli Orti 50t & m; /Agora Museum
Athens/Dagli Orti 58t; /Gianni Dagli Orti 59b, 96t;
/Olympia Museum Greece/Dagli Orti 72bl; /Neil
Setchfield 91t; /Museo Tosio Martinengo Brescia/ Dagli
Orti (A) 93t; /Musée Thomas Dobrée Nantes/Dagli
Orti 94t; /Archaeological Museum Izmir/ Dagli Orti
94b; /Archaeological Museum Salonica/Dagli Orti 95t;
/Archaeological Museum Châtillon-sur- Seine/Dagli Orti
97t; /Archaeological Museum Syracuse 116t; /Museo
Capitolino Rome/Alfredo Dagli Orti 117t; /Museo
Nazionale Taranto/Dagli Orti 121t; /Chiaramonti
Museum Vatican/Dagli Orti (A) 122tr; /Museo
Capitolino Rome/ Dagli Orti (A) 122bl; /Archaeological
Museum Salonica/ Dagli Orti 125t

The Bridgeman Archive: /Museo Archeologico
Nazionale, Naples, Italy 33b; /© Birmingham Museums
and Art Galley 63t; /© Ashmolean Museum, University
of Oxford, UK 72tr; /Private Collection, © The Fine Art
Society, London, UK 78b; /Galleria degli Uffizi,
Florence, Italy, Alinari 79b; /Palazzo Vecchio (Palazzo
della Signoria) Florence, Italy 87t; /Louvre, Paris, France,
Lauros/ Giraudon 90t, 98t; /Museo Capitolino, Rome,
Italy, Giraudon 93b; /Louvre, Paris, France, Giraudon
96b; /Private Collection 103tl, 125b; /Galleria degli
Uffizi, Florence, Italy, Alinari 111t; /Stapleton
Collection, UK, 112t; /British Museum, London, UK
119b; /Private Collection, Archives Charmet 119t

Werner Forman Agency: /Christie's, London 88b;
/Museo Ostia, Italy 88t

Medioimages/Photodisc/Discover Greece/Getty Images:
16br, 29b, 42t, 54t, 61t, 112t

Sylvia Kapp: 24tr, 51t, 75b, 105t, 116bl, 126t, 127b

Mary Evans Picture Library: 108, 109b, 124t

Photo12.com: /Oronoz 2, 22tl, 31b, 47t, 55b, 68t, 70,
85t, 90b, 95b, 115t, 120t; /Ann Ronan Picture Library
5.5, 82–3; /Albert Arnaud 8t, 20t, 100tr, 118t; /Oasis
9b, 24br; /ARJ 27t, 57t, 102b; /Bertelsmann Lexikon
Verlag 56tr; /JTB Photo 56bl, 80t & b, 86b; /Société
Française de Photographie 117b

Frances Reynolds: 128b

CONTENTS

INTRODUCTION

The Parthenon, most famous of all Greek temples, rises supremely above the city of Athens. Epitomizing classical Greece, it was built by the world's first true democracy. The Greeks passionately sought perfection in their politics and in their art. Their achievements in both mark the start of Western history. To this day, men and women fight and die for democracy (a Greek word).

Democracy was not attained or defended just with words or ideas, much though Greeks loved both. Greeks had to fight for their freedom against internal and external enemies. Greatest of outside enemies was the Persian Empire, the world's first superpower, which stretched from the Aegean to northern India. Its rise and fall coincided roughly with Athens' achievement of democracy. In the great conflict of the Persian Wars, the fragmented, usually divided Greek states (around 1,000 scattered from Spain to Cyprus) united to repel the Persian superpower. The major battles of those wars – Marathon, Thermopylae, Salamis and Plataea – are among the pivotal contests in human history. If Persia had won, Greek history and so all western history, would have been very different.

But the Greeks never united again. Instead, they fought each other unceasingly, until finally they fell to other powers: first Macedonia under Philip II and Alexander the Great, then more permanently to Rome. But in their brief centuries of independence, the Greeks experimented constantly, trying out every form of government: democracy, monarchy, dictatorship, oligarchy, even communism (on the Aeolian Islands, near Sicily). In doing so, they invented philosophy and history besides politics in the modern sense. Reading Greek history entails far more than reading about ancient battles: it means rediscovering our political and intellectual origins.

Left: The buildings on the Athenian Acropolis, such as the Erechtheum, still proclaim the achievements of classical Greece at its democratic zenith.

THE MILITARY GREEKS

Our world began with Greece – the world, that is, of Western civilization. The ancient Greeks were the first in so many things that we reveal our debt to them almost every time we open our mouths. Anarchy, astronomy, athletics, ballet, biography, biology, comedy, democracy, diplomacy, drama, ecology, economics, eroticism, history, marathon, maths, music, oligarchy, philosophy, physics, poetry, strategy tactics, technology, theatre, tragedy, tyranny, zoology – all are Greek words. They describe concepts or activities that, while they were not always invented by Greeks, were developed by them into forms we now recognize. Without the ancient Greeks, our modern world would not exist.

Greek civilization reached its zenith in classical Athens, a very small city by modern standards. It did so quickly – in less than 200 years (c.500–300BC) – but the impact has lasted millennia. Nothing like this intensity of experimentation had ever been seen before. Arguably, nothing that the world has seen since has wholly matched it either.

THE FIRST DEMOCRACIES
The Greeks created the world's first democracies, now the officially preferred form of government the world over. Democracy meant rule by all the people, a genuine revolution in human history. There was little in the world of the Mediterranean and Middle East c.600BC, where absolute monarchies and priestly hierarchies were the norm, to suggest that this was about to happen.

But in Greece, hereditary monarchy was dying out or had already been replaced by aristocracies or tyrants (meaning unconstitutional rulers with broad popular support, not necessarily dictators), while there was never a separate priesthood. Even more crucial perhaps, in the Classical Age (c.500–c.300BC) Greece was never unified into a large centrally controlled state, remaining divided into scores of fiercely independent city-states.

This was partly due to geography. Lacking large river valleys or plains, Greece is divided by mountains into small valleys, which inherently encouraged such individualism. But the results made Greek civilization, as it developed focused on each *polis*, crucially different from all earlier civilizations. No one had really done politics (our word comes from *polis*) before the Greeks took to arguing and experimenting, at times violently, about the best forms of government.

LABORATORIES FOR HUMANKIND
Pericles, the supreme democratic states-man of Athens, declared in his funeral oration in 431BC: "Everyone is interested not only in their own affairs but in public

Above: Standing high above the sea, the temple to Poseidon at Sunium, built c.440BC, signalled to ships that they were nearing Athens, the Greek city where democracy and classical art both reached their zenith.

Left: The theatre was among the most typical Greek buildings. The theatre at Epidaurus, dating from the 4th century BC, is remarkably well preserved with still marvellous acoustics.

Left: The Greeks spread from their original homeland in the Greek peninsula and islands, first across the Aegean, then around the Mediterranean and Black Sea, and finally across Asia, founding independent cities as they went.

affairs too, and is well informed about politics. We think that the man who minds only his own business has no business in the city. We Athenians personally decide or discuss policies." (The Greek word *idiot* meant someone who chose a private life – an idiotic choice for Greeks.) With life lived at such intensity, Greek cities became laboratories for humankind.

The Victorian philosopher J.S. Mill declared that the Battle of Marathon in 490BC – when Athens first defeated Persia – was of greater importance in *British* history than the Battle of Hastings. Without that victory, Athenian democracy might not have survived. And without democracy, Athens' open society could not have prospered, encouraging theatre, philosophy, science, history, architecture, art and drama.

Greek democracy had, however, definite limits: women were excluded from public life – as in almost all cultures and countries before the 20th century – and slavery was an essential part of Greek life. But almost every civilization, at the time, and for long after, relied on slaves, and slavery in Athens remained mostly domestic and small-scale.

A worse criticism of the Greeks would be their endless wars. It was the dark side of the Greeks' pursuit of perfection. Just enough city-states united to repel the Persian invasions of 490–478BC, but that unity proved unique. The Greeks reverted to fighting each other, often calling in outside powers – even Persia – to help. Such disunity led at last to their conquest, first by the Macedonians, then by the Romans.

Below: Delphi was the holiest Greek shrine, considered the centre of the world and sacred to the god Apollo. Its oracle, always deliberately enigmatic, was revered by all Greeks.

TIMELINE

Above: The Parthenon, the supreme Greek temple, still rises above Athens despite the vicissitudes of 2,500 years.

Greece has one of the longest histories in the world. The origins of Classical Greece, that supremely accomplished civilization of the 5th and 4th centuries BC, lie in misty prehistory. Archaeology and legend are at first our sole guides, for history proper begins only *c*.550BC. (All dates before 550BC are approximate.) Around 2000BC, as Europe's first civilization emerged on Crete, ancestors of the Greeks appeared in the Greek peninsula and archipelago. By 1200BC they had created the Mycenaean civilization, a dynamic, resplendent culture that later generations peopled with heroes, unaware that a Dark Age, illiterate and impoverished, lay between them. The Greek age proper began with the first Olympic Games, traditionally held in 776BC. From then on Greek life accelerated, reaching its undoubted climax between 500 and 300BC, the age of the Persian Wars, Pericles, Socrates, the great dramatists and generals. But Greek history continued to develop long after Alexander the Great's death in 323BC, becoming linked with that of Rome, its political conqueror but cultural captive. Even the fall of Rome in AD476 merely eclipsed Greek brilliance, which re-emerged in the 15th century to bedazzle the Renaissance.

3000–700BC

3000BC Beginnings of Minoan civilization.
2000BC Building of first palaces in Crete; destruction of Bronze Age Lerna.
1700BC Destruction of first palaces in Crete; start of Second Palatial Period.
1600BC Beginnings of Mycenaean civilization in mainland Greece.
1570BC Palaces in Crete rebuilt after earthquake; Minoan culture at its zenith.
1550BC First shaft-graves at Mycenae.
1500–1470BC Volcanic eruption on Thira devastates Minoan civilization.
1450BC Mycenaeans occupy Knossos.
1380BC Final destruction of Knossos; Mycenaean trade and influence spread.
1300–1250BC Building of Treasury of Atreus, Lion Gate at Mycenae.
1287BC Battle of Cadesh between Egypt and Hittites.
1200BC Destruction of palace at Pylos.
1190BC Traditional date of Trojan War; Egypt repels the Sea Peoples.
1150BC Final collapse of Mycenaean civilization; start of Greek Dark Ages.
1050BC Dorian migrations into Greece; Ionian migration to Asia Minor.
900–800BC Rise of aristocracies in Greece.
776BC First Olympiad (Olympic Games).
760–730BC Homer composes *The Iliad* and *The Odyssey*; adaptation of Phoenician alphabet by Greeks.
753BC Founding of city of Rome.
750BC Foundation of Cumae in Italy, first Greek colony in west.
735BC Foundation of the first Greek colonies in Sicily at Naxos (Catania) and Syracuse.
730–710BC Sparta's first conquest of Messenia.
700BC Hesiod writes *Work and Days* and *Theognis*; according to tradition Deioces founds Median kingdom; introduction of hoplite-style fighting.

699–500BC

682BC List of annual *archons* at Athens begins; Gyges seizes Lydian throne.
669BC Sparta defeated by Argos under King Pheidion.
660BC Lycurgan reforms in Sparta; it crushes Messenian revolt.
***c*.650BC** Rise of tyrants across Greece.
632BC Cylon tries to seize power in Athens; first colony in Libya at Cyrene.
620BC Dracon's Law Code published in Athens; foundation of Byzantium on Bosphorus, Naucratis in Egypt.
612BC Fall of Nineveh, Assyrian capital; first Black Sea colonies (Istrus, Olbia, etc).
***c*.600BC** Thrasybulus tyrant of Miletus; Ionian Enlightenment; first triremes; Sappho, Pittacus and Alcaeus in Lesbos.
594BC Legislation of Solon in Athens.
589BC Foundation of Acragas in Sicily.
585BC Eclipse of sun, predicted by Thales, halts battle between Media and Lydia.
561BC Pisistratus seizes power in Athens; Croesus becomes king of Lydia.
550BC Achaemenid Empire of Persia founded by Cyrus the Great; Sparta forms the Peloponnesian League.
546BC Cyrus conquers Lydia; Sparta defeats Argos, annexes Thyreatis.
538BC Cyrus captures Babylon; he liberates the Jews.
527BC Pisistratus dies; succeeded by sons Hippias and Hipparchus.
514BC Harmodius and Aristogeiton kill Hipparchus; Persian expedition crosses the Danube.
510BC Hippias expelled from Athens with Spartan help.
508BC Cleisthenes' reforms in Athens.
507BC The Spartan invasion under Cleomones is repelled; Athens defeats Boeotians and Chalcidians, and gains Chalcidian territory.

499–450BC

499BC Outbreak of Ionian Revolt.

494BC Defeat of Ionians at Lade by Persia; fall of Miletus; Sparta defeats Argos.

490BC Athenians defeat Persian invasion at Marathon.

487BC First recorded use of ostracism at Athens; *archons* appointed by lot.

486BC Death of Darius the Great of Persia: accession of Xerxes.

483BC New silver lode found at Laurium: Themistocles wins debate on building fleet; Persians dig canal through Mt Athos.

481BC League of Corinth formed to resist Persia under Spartan leadership.

480BC Second Persian invasion under command of Xerxes; August battles of Thermopylae and Artemisium; Athens occupied by the Persians; September Battle of Salamis: Persian fleet destroyed; Carthaginian attack defeated at Himera.

479BC Persians under Mardonius defeated at Plataea by Spartan-led army; Persian fleet defeated at Mycale; revolt of Ionia.

478BC Sparta withdraws from Greek alliance; formation of the League of Delos.

474BC Greeks defeat Etruscans at Cumae.

470BC Birth of Socrates.

467BC Battle of Eurymedon: last Persian fleet destroyed by Athens.

464BC Earthquake at Sparta; *helot* revolt.

463BC Cimon leads Athenian force to help suppress Messenians.

462BC Democratic reforms of Ephialtes.

460BC Outbreak of war between Sparta and Athens; pay for jurors introduced.

459BC Athens sends fleet to help Egyptian revolt against Persia.

458BC *Zeugitae* admitted to *archonship*; building of Long Walls of Athens.

457BC Athens conquers Boeotia.

454BC Loss of Egyptian expedition; Confederacy Treasury moved to Athens.

449–415BC

449BC Peace of Callias with Persia; Athens invites the Greeks to restore her temples.

447BC Parthenon begun; Athens loses Boeotia.

446BC 30 Years' Peace with Sparta (actually to 431BC).

443BC Ostracism of Thucydides, son of Melesias, confirms Pericles' supremacy.

438BC Gold and ivory giant statue of Athena set up in Parthenon.

436BC Foundation of Amphipolis by Athens.

432BC Defensive alliance of Athens with Corcyra; Megarian Decree passed.

431BC Outbreak of Peloponnesian War; invasion of Attica by Peloponnesian army.

430BC Outbreak of plague devastates Athens; Pericles tried and fined.

429BC Pericles reinstated and dies; birth of Plato.

427BC Revolt of Lesbos crushed: debate on how to treat prisoners in Athens.

425BC Athenians occupy Pylos and capture Spartans on Sphacteria: Sparta sues unsuccessfully for peace.

424BC Battle of Delium: Athenians defeated in Boeotia; loss of Amphipolis to Spartan general Brasidas leads to banishment of Thucydides; Congress of Gela in Sicily: Hermocrates propounds 'Monroe Doctrine' for Sicily.

422BC Battle of Amphipolis: deaths of Cleon and Brasidas.

421BC Peace of Nicias.

420BC Alcibiades dominates Assembly.

418BC Battle of Mantinea: Athens and Argos defeated by Sparta.

416BC Athens captures and sacks Melos: 'Melian Debate'.

415BC Mutilation of Herms: Syracusan expedition sails; Alcibiades, recalled to face trial, escapes to Sparta.

414–390BC

414BC Sparta reopens war with Athens; sends Gylippus to help Syracusans.

413BC Spartans occupy fort of Deceleia; Demosthenes sent to Syracuse with reinforcements; great battle in Syracuse harbour; disastrous loss of expedition.

412BC Revolt of Athenian allies; Treaty of Miletus between Sparta and Persia.

411BC Oligarchic revolution at Athens; moderate oligarchy proposed.

410BC Battle of Cyzicus leads to restoration of full democracy in Athens.

409BC Carthage invades Greek Sicily.

408BC Athenians under Alcibiades recapture Byzantium and Chalcedon.

407BC Alcibiades returns to Athens; Prince Cyrus comes down to the Aegean.

406BC Alcibiades leaves Athens after defeat at Notion; Battle of Arginusae; Acragas besieged by Carthaginians; death of playwright Euripides.

405BC Lysander, Spartan *navarch*, defeats Athenian fleet at Aegospotami; end of Athenian power, and blockade of Athens; Dionysius I becomes tyrant of Syracuse.

404BC Surrender of Athens; Long Walls pulled down; dictatorship of the 30.

403BC Spartan garrison on Acropolis; Thrasybulus seizes Piraeus; restoration of democracy, and general amnesty.

401BC 'March of the 10,000' behind Cyrus into Persian Empire; Cyrus killed at Cunaxa; Xenophon leads Greeks home.

399BC Trial and execution of Socrates.

397BC Dionysius I captures Motya in Sicily; Sparta makes truce with Persia.

395BC Athens rebuilding Long Walls.

394BC Thebes, Corinth and Athens Army beaten by Spartans at Battle of Corinth.

393BC Athens completes her Long Walls.

390BC Iphicrates defeats Spartans with light-armed *peltasts*.

389–340BC

386BC The King's Peace: Sparta abandons Ionians in return for Persian support.

382BC Spartans seize Cadmaea (citadel) of Thebes and install pro-Spartan oligarchy.

379BC Spartans expelled from Cadmaea; revolution in Thebes led by Epaminondas.

378BC Athens forms 2nd Confederacy.

376BC Timotheus defeats Spartan fleet at Naxos; Mausolus *satrap* of Caria; Jason of Pherae establishes rule in Thessaly.

371BC Thebes routs Spartans at Leuctra but is checked by Jason.

370BC Assassination of Jason of Pherae; Epaminondas marches into Peloponnese.

369BC Foundation of Messene and liberation of *helots* by Thebans.

367BC Death of Dionysius I of Syracuse, succeeded by Dionysius II.

362BC Epaminondas killed at Mantinea; 'Revolt of the Satraps' against Persian king.

359BC Accession of Philip II of Macedon; defeats invading tribes; accession of Artaxerxes III, dynamic Persian king.

357BC Philip captures Amphipolis and marries Olympias; Dion returns to Sicily and 'liberates' Syracuse; start of the Athens' War of the Allies.

356BC Philomelus of Phocis seizes Delphi, starting Sacred War; Philip captures Potidaea; birth of Alexander.

354BC Murder of Dion in Syracuse; Athens makes peace with allies. Onomarchus of Phocis defeats Philip;

353BC Philip captures Methone; death of Mausolus of Halicarnassus.

352BC Philip defeats Phocians and becomes *tagus* (ruler) of Thessaly.

347BC Death of Plato.

346BC Peace of Philocrates ends Sacred War: Philip as protector of Delphi.

340BC Philip attacks Byzantium; Alexander left as regent of Macedonia.

339–327BC

338BC Battle of Chaeronea: Theban and Athenian armies defeated by Philip; death of Isocrates, Athenian orator; murder of Artaxerxes III by Bagoas, his Vizier.

337BC Council of Corinth elects Philip General of the Greeks for anti-Persian crusade; death of Timoleon in Sicily.

336BC Macedonian advance guard sent to Asia; Philip II murdered; accession of Alexander III; swift descent on Greece, where he is proclaimed General; accession of Darius III in Persia.

335BC Alexander campaigns in Thrace; Alexander's destruction of Thebes; Aristotle begins teaching at Athens.

334BC Alexander crosses into Asia; defeats Persians at Battle of Granicus; liberates Ionia; sieges of Miletus and Halicarnassus.

333BC Alexander cuts Gordian Knot; death of Greek mercenary general Memnon; change in Persian tactics; Battle of Issus (November): Alexander routs Persians; Darius flees east.

332BC Siege of Tyre (January–July); siege of Gaza; Alexander enters Egypt.

331BC Foundation of city of Alexandria; trip to consult oracle at Siwah; Alexander routs Persians at Gaugamela; enters Babylon and Susa; Sparta defeated by Macedonia.

330BC Alexander burns Persepolis; Darius murdered by Bessus; Alexander executes Philotas and Parmenion.

329BC Alexander crosses Hindu Kush to Bactria; crosses River Oxus; founds Alexandria Eschate; winters in Bactria.

328BC Campaign against Spitamenes; Alexander quarrels with and kills Cleitus.

327BC Capture of Sogdian Rock; Alexander marries Roxane; tries to introduce Persian *proskynesis*; Pages' Conspiracy – Callisthenes executed; enters India at the end of the year.

326–278BC

326BC Alexander defeats Porus at Hydaspes; conquers Punjab; advance to River Beas, where troops mutiny; forced to turn back.

325BC Conquest of the Malli: Alexander almost fatally wounded; he sails down Indus to Ocean; marches through Gedrosian Desert with many fatalities; voyage of Nearchus along coast.

324BC Execution of corrupt *satraps*; Susa weddings of Persians and Macedonians; mutiny of discharged veterans at Opis; Exiles Decree at Olympia; death of Hephaistion (October).

323BC Alexander enters Babylon; Greek cities hail him as a god; Alexander dies on 10 June; wars of the Diadochi (successors) and Lamian War of the Greeks against Macedonia; revolt of colonists in Bactria.

322BC Ptolemy gains control of Egypt: Lamian War ends in Greek defeat by Antipater; deaths of Demosthenes and Aristotle; Athenian democracy curtailed.

312BC Seleucus I takes over eastern *satrapies*; founds Seleucia-on-the-Tigris.

303BC Seleucus cedes Indian territories in return for 500 elephants.

301BC Battle of Ipsus: death of Antigonus I and division of world into four kingdoms.

300BC Zeno sets up Stoic School in Athens; Seleucus founds Antioch in Syria.

297BC Pyrrhus I king of Epirus (to 272BC).

295BC Library at Alexandria founded.

283BC Death of Ptolemy I, founder of Ptolemaic dynasty, in Egypt.

280BC Seleucus I defeats and kills Lysimachus, ending his kingdom, then murdered himself; Antiochus I succeeds him (to 261).

280–275BC Pyrrhus fights Romans in Italy without success; foundation of Achaean League in southern Greece.

279BC Building of Pharos at Alexandria.

274–200BC

274–232BC Reign of Ashoka, first Buddhist emperor, in India.

270BC Hieron emerges as saviour of Syracuse, assuming crown as Hieron II.

263–41BC Eumenes I of Pergamum starts to assert independence from Seleucids.

264BC First Punic War between Carthage and Rome starts.

*c.***255BC** Bactria breaks away from Seleucid control, followed by Parthia.

245–213BC Aratus dominates Achaean League, seizes Corinth (243BC).

244BC Agis IV (to 241) tries to introduce radical reforms at Sparta and is killed.

241BC End of First Punic War: Rome takes over most of Sicily.

235BC Cleomenes III King of Sparta (to 222BC) introduces radical reforms before being defeated; Euthydemnus I seizes power in Bactria and expands kingdom.

230BC Attalus I defeats Gauls.

229BC Athens 'buys out' Macedonian garrison, in effect becoming neutral.

228BC Rome makes Illyria protectorate.

223BC Antiochus III the Great succeeds to Seleucid throne (to 187BC).

221BC Philip V succeeds to Macedonian throne (to 179BC); Ptolemy IV defeats Antiochus III at Raphia 218.

218–202BC Second Punic War.

217BC Peace Conference at Naupactus: warning of the 'shadow of Rome'.

216BC Romans defeated at Cannae.

215BC Alliance of Philip and Carthage leads to First Macedonian War (to 205BC); Syracuse switches support to Hannibal.

212BC Antiochus starts eastern campaigns; fall of Syracuse to Romans: Archimedes killed in the fighting.

202BC Hannibal finally defeated at Zama.

200BC Egypt defeated by Antiochus III at Ionion, loses southern Syria/Palestine.

199–70BC

197BC Macedonia defeated at Battle of Cynoscephalae.

196BC Flaminius declares 'Liberty for Greeks' at Corinth.

192BC Start of 'First Syrian' War of Rome against Antiochus III.

190BC Antiochus defeated at Magnesia.

188BC Treaty of Apamea: Antiochus loses all land west of Taurus mountains.

171–138BC Mithradates I of Parthia expands kingdom at Seleucid expense.

171–168BC Third Macedonian War.

170BC Eucratides I rules united Indo-Greek kingdom (to 155BC).

168BC Perseus of Macedonia defeated at Pydna; Antiochus IV forced to abandon conquest of Egypt; his intervention in Jerusalem sparks Maccabee revolt.

166BC Romans enslave 150,000 Epirotes, make Delos a free port; slave trade booms.

155–130BC Menander, king of huge Indo-Greek kingdom reaching the Ganges, possibly converts to Buddhism.

146BC Romans sack Corinth; make Achaea and Macedonia Roman provinces.

133BC Attalus III of Pergamum dies leaving kingdom to Rome.

130BC Romans crush Aristonicus' Utopian revolt and make Asia Minor a Roman province; Parthians capture Babylonia.

122BC Gauis Gracchus gives tax-farming rights for Asia and Greece to his allies in Rome, leading to ruinous extortion.

120BC Mithradates VI king of Pontus.

88BC Mithradates VI overruns Rome's eastern provinces offering 'liberty' to the Greeks; massacre of 80,000 Italians on Delos and other islands.

86–85BC Sulla sacks Athens.

73BC Lucullus defeats Mithradates and drives him out of Pontus to Crimea, where he commits suicide.

69BC–AD1462

66–63BC Pompey reorganizes the east: Syria and Bithynia-Pontus become provinces, Judaea and others client states.

51BC Parthians invade Syria; Cleopatra becomes co-monarch of Egypt.

48BC Battle of Pharsalus: Pompey flees to Egypt and is killed; Caesar, following, meets Cleopatra and has affair.

47BC Caesar leaves Egypt; Cleopatra later follows him to Rome; Cicero in retirement summarizes Greek philosophy.

44BC Caesar assassinated.

42BC Battle of Philippi: Cassius and Brutus defeated by Antony and Octavian; Antony takes eastern empire; winters in Athens.

41BC Antony meets Cleopatra at Tarsus.

36BC Antony invades Parthia but is forced to retreat.

31BC Battle of Actium: Octavian's forces defeat Antony and Cleopatra.

30BC Antony and Cleopatra commit suicide: Egypt annexed to Roman Empire by Octavian; Kushans (Scythians) overrun last Indo-Greek kingdom.

AD14 Death of Augustus (Octavian), first Roman emperor; succeeded by Tiberius.

AD66 Nero visits Greece, wins all prizes at the Olympics and declares 'liberty' for Greek cities.

AD124 Hadrian visits Athens and makes it head of Panhellenic League; completes Temple of Olympian Zeus.

AD393 Last Olympic Games held.

AD397–8 Visigoths ravage Greece.

AD529 Justinian closes Academy and other philosophy schools in Athens.

1438 Council of Florence; Bessarion stays on in Italy, rekindling knowledge of Greek.

1453 Fall of Constantinople to Ottoman Turks; some Greek scholars flee to Italy.

1462 Platonist Academy founded in Florence to study Greek philosophy.

Pages 10–13: The coins of ancient Greece were some of the very first ever to be minted. They were often brilliantly decorative, and they remain among the most beautiful and well designed that the world has seen.

CHAPTER I

THE GREEK AWAKENING

c.2000–500BC

Greek history starts far earlier than the Greeks themselves suspected (or anyone else before recent archaeological discoveries). People who were possibly the Greeks' ancestors appeared in the peninsula around 2000BC. At about the same time, and perhaps not by coincidence, the sophisticated Minoan civilization arose in Crete and the Cyclades. While the Minoans were almost certainly not Greek, the Mycenaeans, who took over Crete and were influenced by its culture, definitely were.

Heroic myths cluster around the Mycenaean palaces of the late Bronze Age (1600–1200BC). This suggests that there is a kernel of truth to most Greek legends, although they should not be regarded as history. Greeks of the historical period proper (from *c*.550BC) mostly believed their legends, especially when related by Homer, but they had only the haziest ideas of their actual pre-history. In particular, they were unaware that between them and their legendary ancestors lay the chasm of the Greek Dark Ages. When Greek life revived after 800BC, it took very different forms from Mycenaean Greece.

One factor remained constant, however: the mountainous landscape, with valleys often isolated from each other, meant that Greece remained divided politically into many small, even tiny states. This helped to give Greek life its passionate intensity centred on the *polis*, the citizen-state.

Left: The huge grave shafts of Mycenae – "rich in gold" according to Homer – are the first Greek buildings, dating to c.1550BC.

MINOAN CRETE
THE FIRST CIVILIZATION 2000–1100BC

Above: This figurine, bare-breasted in the courtly Minoan fashion, represents the earth-goddess or possibly one of her priestesses.

Europe's first civilization arose in Crete and the Aegean islands during the Bronze Age. It is called Minoan after its legendary king Minos. According to the Athenian historian Thucydides, Minos was the first to rule the seas and islands. Thucydides was long thought to be just repeating myths about the king of Cnossus, who reputedly exacted tribute from Athens: 14 girls and boys to be fed to the Minotaur, the bull-headed monstrous offspring of Minos' wife, Queen Pasiphae, and a bull. But, since Arthur Evans began excavations at Cnossus in 1900, controversially restoring many of the ruins, Thucydides has been proved partly right: there was a great civilization in Crete with outposts across the Aegean.

Cretan civilization started modestly in the 3rd millennium. Around 2000BC the first palaces – multi-storeyed buildings centred on courtyards – were built at Cnossus, Phaestos and Mallia. They were influenced by Egyptian and Near Eastern models, for the Cretans were by then sailing south and east, bringing home ivory and other luxury products in return for jewellery, wine, textiles and olive oil. Egyptian records of the 2nd millennium BC often mention Cretans (as tribute-bearers, although Crete was never a tributary to Egypt), but Minoan civilization soon developed its own highly distinctive characteristics.

A PEACEFUL SOCIETY

Notable among Minoan society's characteristics were its peaceful nature and the prominent role seemingly played by women. However, the Cretans were never total pacifists – they presumably relied mostly on their navy for defence – and ideas of a matriarchy, with women ruling the realm, are probably misplaced. Around 1700BC all the palaces were destroyed by earthquakes.

But, with Minoan culture vigorously resurgent, they were soon rebuilt as larger, even more elegant complexes.

Below: The Minoan Palace at Cnossus with its characteristic dark-red columns.

Above: This vivid fresco of children boxing was found on Thira, the Aegean island devastated by the volcanic eruption in c.1500BC that is thought to have half-wrecked Minoan civilization.

Below: The grand staircase at Cnossus Palace, the largest of the Cretan palaces, reveals the surprisingly modern-looking ingenuity of Minoan architects.

Cretans of the period *c*.1700–1500BC (called Late Minoan by Evans, Later Palatial by others) produced pottery, jewellery and other vivid artworks that can still delight. The palaces, especially the largest at Cnossus, had bathrooms with running water and light-wells. Their buildings had dark red columns tapering downwards and rose four or even five storeys high. On their walls, frescoes depicted a graceful, idyllic life, with bare-breasted women in long flounced dresses and with elaborate hairstyles, and clean-shaven men in kilts, surrounded by flowers, birds and dolphins. A cult of the bull was clearly central to Cretan religion, demonstrated by the many images of bulls and by the bull-dance, a game or rite common on murals. (This may underlie the Minotaur legend.) The axe was also a common motif. Paved roads connected palaces with outlying villages and villas around the island. The population of Cnossus town reached *c*.30,000 by 1500BC, making it the largest Mediterranean city of the age.

Minoan culture was not confined to Crete, however, but also flourished in the Cyclades and some other Aegean islands. Most prosperous was Thira (Santorini), which was probably independent. Murals excavated there show a fleet attacking a walled town and reveal Thira's links with north Africa. But the predominant note, as in Crete, was peaceful. After 1600BC, Minoan culture spread to the mainland, with such strong Minoan influence

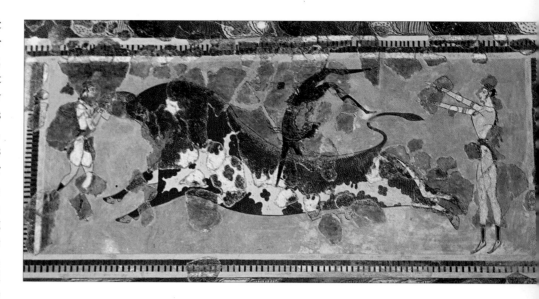

evident in mainland sites that Evans talked of a Minoan Empire. But certainly here the rulers, Mycenaean Greeks, were independent, merely employing Minoan craftsmen to make them precious objects.

THE THIRA ERUPTION
This cheerful civilization was in its prime when an immense volcanic explosion tore Thira apart. It also devastated other islands, including Crete, while preserving part of Thira town under lava like a Bronze Age Pompeii. The date of the eruption remains debated, ranging from 1600BC, the geologists' preferred date, to 1460BC, which suits archaeologists better. Indisputably, when Cnossus Palace was rebuilt *c*.1450BC, it was occupied by Greek-speakers, for clay Linear B tablets written in early Greek have been found there. Although a warlike note emerges in the tablets, Cnossus, 'house of the double axe' (*labyrinth*), remained unwalled.

Then one day *c*.1380BC a fire, caused by accident, earthquake or human attack, gutted the palace once more and it was never rebuilt. Minoan culture now entered its less glorious 'post-palatial' phase. This may not have been totally impoverished – Homer ranked Crete as second only to Mycenae in his 'Catalogue of Ships'. But *c*.1100BC Dorian Greek invaders, who had attacked the Peloponnese already, invaded Crete, finally wrecking the Minoan world.

Above: The cult of the bull was central to Minoan religious life. Bull-leaping, as this fresco reveals, was dangerous. It probably had religious connotations but was conducted insouciantly.

Below: This languid youth is called the Lily Prince. Like most Cretan young men, he wore only a kilt, but he also has an elaborate head-dress.

LINEAR B
Linear B was the third form of writing developed in Crete. The first was a pictographic script, the second was a syllabic system, Linear A, while Linear B was similar but in Greek. Linear B tablets record flocks of sheep, oil jars, horses, spears and chariots, not royal edicts, history or poetry, yet they shed invaluable light on this highly civilized society now ruled by Greek incomers.

MYCENAEAN SOCIETY
THE FIRST GREEKS, 1600–1200 BC

Above: The Lion Gate, erected c.1300BC, still guards the entrance to Mycenae. Its massive walls so impressed later Greeks that they assumed they had been built by Cyclops, one-eyed giants.

Below: The Mycenaeans were impressively skilled architects, building corbelled vaults. The 'Treasury of Atreus', which dates from c.1300BC, is not really a treasury but a tomb.

In the 3rd millennium BC a prosperous Bronze Age culture developed in the Greek peninsula in small unwalled towns such as Lerna in the Peloponnese. Around 2000BC these were destroyed by invaders, probably from the north, and for a time urban life totally disappeared. Then *c.*1600 BC a new civilization emerged that built amazing tombs at Mycenae in the north-west Peloponnese filled with so many gold artefacts that Homer's epithet "Mycenae, rich in gold" is justified. This was probably due to the rise of powerful new kings, not fresh invasions, but nothing is known about them.

In Greek legend, including Homer's great poems *The Iliad* and *The Odyssey* written in the 8th century BC, Mycenae was the paramount kingdom, so this first Greek civilization has been called Mycenaean. But Achaean, the term used by both Homer and by contemporary Hittite kings in Anatolia who had diplomatic dealings with them, is more apposite. Nothing suggests that Bronze Age Greece was politically united under Mycenae, although it probably controlled the Argolid plain beneath its citadel, from which paved roads radiated.

MYCENAEAN CULTURE EMERGES
In the 16th century BC the cultural influence of Minoan Crete, then far more sophisticated, was overwhelming on the Mycenaeans. Superb gold cups found near Sparta, showing bulls being tethered by long-haired youths, reveal this. But already distinctive themes favoured by Mycenaeans, such as hunting and warfare, were emerging. The early (*c.*1600BC) gold mask from Grave A at Mycenae shows a fierce bearded warrior most unlike clean-shaven Minoans. After 1460BC Greek warriors, possibly from Mycenae, occupied the palace at Cnossus after the Thira eruption.

Among cultural imports from Crete was writing in Linear B, subsequently adopted in Mycenaean centres. These include nearby Tiryns, Thebes and Orchomenus in central Greece, Athens (although it remained of secondary importance) and Pylos in the south-west Peloponnese. Excavations at Pylos have unearthed a complete Mycenaean palace, with elegant tapering columns and murals depicting hippogriffs and other mythical figures. Uniquely, Pylos was unwalled. Linear B tablets found there reveal a bureaucracy trying to control almost every aspect of daily life. Mycenaean culture spread north into Thessaly, across the Aegean to Miletus on the Asian shore and east to Cyprus. There was probably a palace near Sparta in the fertile Eurotas valley, but none has been found.

PROTECTING MYCENAE
Mycenaean wealth grew throughout the 14th century BC. It probably came from both trading and raiding – piracy, Thucydides noted, was socially perfectly acceptable in legendary times. Greek artefacts, mainly pottery, have been found as far west as Sicily and as far east as Syria. Mycenaean outposts replaced Minoans

SCHLIEMANN AND TROY

In the 19th century, scholars dismissed Homer's epic and other Greek myths as just that: pure invention, with no historical foundation. Ancient Greeks, who had treated such legends as fact, were considered to have been childishly naïve. Considered equally naïve, therefore, was German business-man Heinrich Schliemann (1822–90), who had been fascinated by Greek legends since childhood. Convinced that Homer had not invented the Trojan wars, Schliemann began excavating the site in north-west Turkey reputed to be Troy. He discovered nine superimposed cities, and in 1873 found a treasure that he declared was the Trojan king Priam's. In fact, it was much older. In 1876 he turned to Mycenae and soon struck gold there too – literally, for he found himself looking at the gold death mask of a Bronze Age king. "I have looked on the face of Agamemnon," he declared. Again, he was out by centuries, but he had convinced the world that legendary Greece had existed in some form.

after 1400BC, but the Mycenaeans soon ventured further north than Cretans had ever sailed.

To protect Mycenae against threats from abroad or at home, massive new walls were built around its citadel, incorporating the earlier grave circles. The towering Lion Gate, with two lions flanking a pillar, dominated the new approach. Below, houses belonging to

nobles, craftsmen and traders made up a little city. Most palaces had a pillared *megaron* (throne-room), but few reveal much evidence of planning.

THE ENIGMA OF TROY

Up by the Hellespont (Dardanelles) the Mycenaeans found the ancient trading city of Troy, controlling trade routes from the Black Sea, a good enough cause for war. The Trojan War, that epic ten-year siege variously estimated to have occurred between 1250 and 1190BC, remains one of archaeology's enigmas. There *was* a city destroyed around there and then, Troy VIIA, and recent excavations have shown that this was larger than once thought, with impressive palaces. Perhaps a Greek army led by Agamemnon, king of Mycenae, did besiege Troy to retrieve Helen, the Spartan king's beautiful wife abducted by the Trojan prince Paris, as recounted in Homer's *Iliad*. Or perhaps it did not. But the 13th century certainly ended in general wars. Mycenaean civilization, top-heavy, collapsed soon after.

Above: The gold mask that Heinrich Schliemann, the enthusiastic rediscoverer of Troy and Mycenae, called the Mask of Agamemnon is in fact far earlier than the Trojan Wars, dating from the 16th century BC. Its still half-barbaric splendour indicates that the lords of Mycenae had already grown rich, whether this wealth was from trading, raiding or fighting as mercenaries.

Left: The Minoans' cultural influence on the mainland Greeks was for a time overwhelming. This gold cup, found at Vaphio, near Sparta, and dating from the 16th century BC, is Minoan both in its naturalistic style and its bull-taming theme.

Above: Ephesus was among the greatest of the Ionian cities of Asia Minor, traditionally founded by the Ionians fleeing from the Doric invasions around 1000BC.

THE DARK AGES
1200–800BC

Around the year 1200BC almost all the major Mycenaean centres were destroyed by unknown attackers despite their strengthened fortifications. Some sites, such as Pylos, were abandoned, fires baking their Linear B tablets enduringly hard for posterity. Only Athens, secure on its rock thanks to a covered passage running down to a secret well, survived intact. (In legend this survival was due to the self-sacrifice of Codrus, its last king, who thus fulfilled a prophecy that the city would be saved if its king were killed. After such a heroic death, Athens becamean aristocratic republic.) But its status as the one unsacked city reinforced subsequent Athenian beliefs that they alone were autochthonic (sprung from the land), unlike the Dorian newcomers.

Later Greeks remembered the upheavals at the end of the Mycenaean age as the 'return of the Heraclids' (sons of Heracles or Hercules – a Mycenaean prince) to reclaim their inheritance two generations after the Trojan War. They failed to realize that there had been a complete break between the elaborate, literate world of the Bronze Age palaces and much simpler later societies. The break was not sudden – Mycenae itself was briefly reoccupied and there were actually some new settlements along the east coast of Attica. But what followed was a true Dark Age: illiterate, isolated and impoverished.

MYCENEAN REFUGEES
According to legend, Dorian tribes entered Greece from the north-west, a region untouched by Mycenaean culture, and moved down into the Peloponnese, destroying as they went. Refugees from the kingdom of Pylos sailed first to impregnable Athens and then across the seas to found new cities on the Asian coast such as Smyrna and Ephesus, soon called Ionian. Some Mycenaeans sailed further east to untouched Cyprus, where they maintained a fading Bronze Age lifestyle, complete with chariots and a

Right: By 800BC Greece had become linguistically divided into groups, whose culture as well as dialect were distinctive. Foremost among these groups were Ionian, spoken in Athens, the islands and Ionia, and Doric, spoken in Sparta, Crete and Rhodes.

simplified syllabic alphabet, down to the time of the Persian Wars (499–478BC). Others retreated into Arcadia, the mountainous heart of the Peloponnese, where they preserved their own independence, dialect and customs, albeit in rustic form.

Another explanation for the collapse of Mycenaean civilization is climate change – perhaps a prolonged drought – but there certainly were large migrations and invasions in the years after 1200.

THE DIALECTS OF GREECE

The main reason for accepting in outline the tradition of northern invaders is linguistic. While all Mycenaean Greeks seem to have spoken much the same language (judging by Linear B tablets), in historic Greece there were several major linguistic divisions. In much of the Peloponnese, including the Corinthian Isthmus (though not inland Arcadia), in Crete, Rhodes and some southern Cyclades, the Dorian dialect became the norm. Dorian Greek was in some ways old-fashioned – the *a* in *phrater* (brother) remained long, for example, while it became short in other dialects. In Attica, including Athens, the island of Euboea, many of the Cyclades, most east Aegean islands and many cities on the east coast, people spoke Ionic Greek. This became the language (in grandly poetic form) of Homer, greatest of all Greek poets, in the 8th century BC.

In central Greece – Boeotia and Thessaly, on the large island of Lesbos and the adjacent northern Asian coastline, all colonized from central Greece, Aeolic, a form of Greek closer to Ionian than Dorian emerged, which influenced the language of Hesiod, the second great Greek poet. Another dialect, now called North-western Greek, was spoken appropriately in north-western Greece, while modern scholars, recognizing the similarity between the Greek of the Arcadians and that of the Cypriots, have identified a separate Arcado-Cypriot dialect. This was not, however, recognized at the time. Although there were definite cultural as well as linguistic differences between the

dialect-speakers, all could understand each other well enough – when they wanted to.

FRESH BEGINNINGS

Clues to new developments in this illiterate society come mostly from pottery, whose shards have survived. At first potters continued to produce feebler versions of the ornate Mycenaean 'palace' styles, but *c*.1050BC a wholly new style emerged in Athens called Protogeometric. Radically simple, content with almost abstract designs and not concerned to fill every empty space, it ranks as perhaps the first truly Hellenic art. (The Greeks now began calling themselves Hellenes: 'Greek' is a Roman word.) Over the next three centuries Geometric art, using stark zigzags and triangles, developed more elaborate shapes but remained stylized. Clothing, too, changed around 1100BC, with simple Dorian cloaks replacing elaborate Mycenaean-style clothes. Almost all buildings were now made of timber, with small thatched cottages serving as temples, befitting a society hardly above subsistence level, ruled by local lords hardly richer than the peasants working for them. Few men looked far afield.

Above: In tradition and probably in reality, Athens was the 'unsacked city' that alone survived the Dorian invasions, perpetuating Mycenaean traditions.

Below: The far simpler way of life that emerged in Greece's Dark Ages (1200–800BC) resulted in a new, simpler style of pottery: Protogeometric and then, as in this 8th-century BC amphora, Geometric.

THE GREEK RENAISSANCE
800–700 BC

Above: The stories of Odysseus' wanderings, so magnificently related by Homer, gave generations of potters themes. Here Odysseus is bound to the mast of his ship to resist the fatally alluring song of the Sirens.

Below: Mt Olympus, the highest mountain in Greece and often cloud-capped, was the mythical home of the 12 Olympian gods. It also marked the northern frontier of Greece proper.

Around 800BC this enclosed, static society began to change. The spur was increasing population, growing (if still modest) prosperity at home and renewed contacts with traders from the Levant. The traders were Phoenicians, a Semitic people from the coasts of modern Lebanon who founded Carthage near modern Tunis in 814BC. The use of iron also spread, giving Greek farmers metal axes, ploughs and other useful implements. But Greek society remained essentially aristocratic, meaning ruled by *aristoi* (the best), as hereditary nobles modestly called themselves.

THE GREEK ALPHABET
Eastern influences first appear in art, depicting human beings and animals, often mythical such as sphinxes, in freer if not yet realistic ways. But the greatest single change was the revival of literacy. Around 770BC some Greeks, probably poets, adopted the Phoenician alphabet,

Above: Olympia in the Peloponnese emerged as one of the holiest sites in the Greek world in the 8th century BC, famed for its quadrennial games, the greatest in the Greek calendar, and later for its temple housing an enormous statue of Zeus.

adding the vowels needed for Greek to make 24 letters and adjusting the symbols. Semitic *aleph* became Greek *alpha*, the first letter. More flexible and easier to learn than the 300-character Mycenaean system, the new alphabet spread around the Greek world. Our own Roman alphabet derives directly from it. One of the first uses of literacy was to record the works of Homer, the greatest Greek poet.

HOMER'S *ILIAD* AND *ODYSSEY*
There are no reliable details about Homer's life. He probably lived *c.*750BC on the island of Chios or the adjacent Ionian mainland, and traditionally was blind. Whether the two great Homeric poems, *The Iliad* and *The Odyssey*, were written by the same man remains debated. Homer's theme in *The Iliad* is the wrath of Prince Achilles and its disastrous effects on the last stages of the ten-year Trojan War, of which, however, he gives only fleeting glimpses. In this grand tragedy he lauded heroic values such as *philotimon* (love of honour), *areté*

(meaning variously courage, excellence, perfection), endurance and a fiercely competitive individualism.

By contrast, in *The Odyssey*, his adventure-story-cum-comedy, Odysseus triumphs chiefly by craftiness. Homer's description of an aristocratic society led by kings, with the voices of common people such as Thersites firmly ignored, inadvertently mingles current Iron Age customs with those of the Bronze Age. His heroes ride into battle in Mycenaean chariots and carry Bronze Age giant shields, but they are cremated, not buried as Mycenaeans were. Although they live in palaces, these are simply large houses, lacking the bureaucracies and splendours of real Mycenae or Pylos. Queen Penelope, wife of wandering Odysseus, spins her own wool.

Homer's influence on later Greeks has been compared to that of the Bible and Shakespeare combined – or to Hollywood *plus* television today. All Greeks with any education could quote Homer, and he

inspired men as diverse as the philosopher Socrates and Alexander the Great. In portraying the Twelve Olympians (the chief gods on Mt Olympus) light-heartedly as super-sized humans, Homer's writing had a beneficial side effect. If even Zeus, king of the gods, could be portrayed as hen-pecked by his wife Hera, there was small danger of Greeks being totally over-awed by their gods' majesty. (The Greeks never had a special priestly caste or clergy. This helped philosophy– that quest for truth by non-religious means – to spring up in Ionia two centuries later.)

THE WORK OF HESIOD

Balancing the exuberant aristocratic splendour of Homer's world are the *Theognis* and *Works and Days* of Hesiod, a poet who lived slightly later (*c*.700BC) in rural Boeotia, an area noted for its dullness. An independent small farmer, Hesiod grumbles at the rich and at the weather, but provides useful advice to his feckless brother on when to sow and plough. He has a strong distrust of seafaring and a peasant's attitude to accruing more land. In his *Theognis* he gave a systematic genealogy for the gods and an account of divine myths, darker in tone than Homer's, that also proved very influential on later generations.

Above: This vase, dating from 490BC, illustrates a typically combative scene between Achilles and Memnon from Homer's first great poem, The Iliad, *about the Trojan Wars. Homer's poetry swiftly became the basis of Greek culture.*

Below: Almost nothing definite is known about the life of Homer, the supreme Greek poet, but he was reputedly blind. He certainly was an Ionian Greek, for he wrote in the Ionian dialect.

THE FIRST OLYMPICS

Another vital aspect of Greek life emerged in the 8th century BC: the Olympic Games, traditionally first held at Olympia in west Greece in 776BC. At first just a Peloponnesian event, it soon attracted Greek athletes from all over Greece and overseas to its contest held once every four years. For this, the greatest athletic event in the Hellenic world, the forever-warring Greeks observed a rare truce. After an athlete's loincloth fell off, it was decided that all contestants should compete naked, like the gods. The (usually aristocratic) victor at a major contest such as chariot races was hailed as a semi-divine hero by his native city, often having a statue erected to him. At Olympia were created some of the finest temples and statues. Pheidias, the supreme Classical Athenian sculptor, made a huge statue of Zeus there.

THE EXPANSION OF GREECE
750–580BC

Above: The island of Ortygia off the south-eastern Sicilian coast became the kernel of Syracuse, founded in 734BC, ultimately the greatest and most powerful Greek city in the west. These columns of the Temple to Apollo date from the 6th century BC.

Below: Electrum and silver coins of Phocaea (Ionia) in western Anatolia.

Right: Although only founded in c.580BC, Acragas became the richest of Greek Sicilian cities, thanks to its wool trade. Its 'Vale of Temples' included this Temple to Concordia from the prosperous 5th century BC.

By 550BC Greek 'colonies' – that is, autonomous city-states, not dependent territories – stretched across the Mediterranean from southern Gaul (France) to Egypt, with many more around the Black Sea. Southern Italy was so densely settled with Greek cities that the Romans called it *magna Graecia* (greater Greece). This remarkable expansion, which occurred within about two centuries, was driven chiefly by growing land hunger.

The mountainous nature of much of the country meant that the amount of fertile land in Greece was limited. To make matters worse, the Greek custom of dividing inherited land equally between all surviving sons meant that farms often became too small to be viable. (Most Greeks were, of course, farmers.) When the population began to expand in the 8th century BC, the pressure on the available land grew.

THE FIRST COLONIES

In almost every Greek city there were persistent – if unfounded – traditions that in the legendary past a wise ruler had divided up all land equally, and so subsequent inequalities, which benefited aristocrats, were unjust. A redistribution of land was a recurring wish of ordinary people and the nightmare of ruling aristocracies. To avert revolution, cities

Above: Settlers from Megara founded Acragas (modern Agrigento), once Sicily's wealthiest city,

turned to founding colonies overseas, some of which proved very popular, some less so. The colonists sent out *c.*630BC from the small island of Thira to Cyrene in Libya, for example, were forbidden to return within six years no matter what happened. (In fact, Cyrene boomed thanks to its wheat and wool.)

The first colonies were founded *c.*750BC at Cyme and the island of Ischia, near Naples, to obtain the metals Greece lacked. These colonists were soon followed by those from other cities seeking good farmland: Chalcis, from Euboea, founded Naxos, Catania and Rhegium, now Reggio, on the Straits of Messina. Corinth founded Corcyra (Corfu) and in 734BC Syracuse, which was to become the greatest city in the west. The Achaeans of the north Peloponnese founded Sybaris, Croton and Metapontion in southern Italy, all built on prime agricultural land, where they soon grew rich. Even Sparta joined in, founding Taras (Taranto) *c.*700BC.

After a pause, colonies also began founding their own colonies. Megara, a Sicilian offshoot of the Megara that lies north-east of Corinth, sent settlers west to Selinus (Selinunte) *c.*630BC and to Acragas

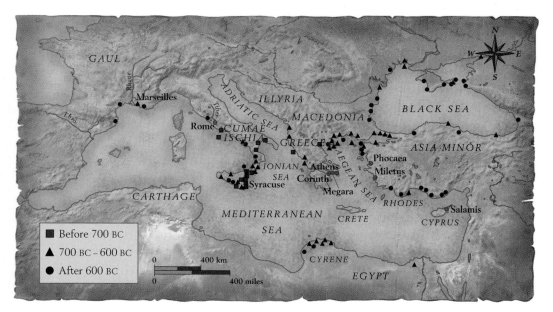

Left: Starting with colonies at Ischia and Cumae around the Bay of Naples in c.750BC, the Greeks founded cities all around the Mediterranean, from the south of France (Marseilles, Antibes and Nice) to Naucratis in the Egyptian Delta, to solve problems of over-population at home.

(Agrigento), later Sicily's wealthiest city, c.580BC. Phocaea, in north Ionia, colonized southern Gaul: Nice, Antibes, Monaco and Marseilles are all in origin Greek. The westernmost Greek city was Emporiae in north-east Spain, a trade centre (as its name suggests). Trade across the whole Greek world grew thanks to such colonization.

New settlers went out not as individuals but in planned groups, at times led by an aristocrat's younger son, sometimes not taking wives with them. Instead, they married local women, often those of native inhabitants they had dispossessed. Not all colonists necessarily came from one city. Small places such as Phocaea recruited landless men from other cities. While most colonies retained strong sentimental ties with their mother city, all were fully independent from the start.

THE CITIZEN-STATE

The *polis*, city-state, was the main political unit of Greece. It is more accurate to call it 'citizen-state', for it meant the body of all politically active men, not its buildings. (Women, slaves and resident foreigners were inhabitants but not active citizens of a *polis*.) A *polis* often had citizens living outside its walls, in villages or small towns, who walked into the city centre. When Athens itself was occupied by invading Persians in 480BC, Themistocles, its leader, was taunted with being cityless. He pointed out that Athens consisted of its assembled citizens, who would sail off and found a new city if the united Greek fleet did not stand and fight. A *polis* was always fiercely autonomous.

THE BLACK SEA

There was wealth to be had in the north-east around the Black Sea, although attempts to establish colonies in the crowded Levant failed, except briefly at Al-Mina in Syria. The three-pronged peninsula of the Chalcidice was first colonized by Chalcis, and then by Megara. Megara went on to found Byzantium (Istanbul) at a superb site on the Bosphorus in 629BC. Beyond lay the wide cold waters of the Black Sea.

Here another host of colonies sprang up: Sinope, Amisus and Trebizond on the south coast, and Olbia, Panticapaeum and Tyrus around the north, in a chilly region the Greeks found strange. The Scythian hinterland (Ukraine) exported grain, gold, timber and slaves in return for Greek oil, wine and artefacts. Wheat from the Black Sea became increasingly important to Greece, especially to Athens. Ultimately, whoever controlled the Black Sea grain supply could throttle Athens.

Below: The Greeks also settled thickly around the shores of the Black Sea, to them a very alien area. They traded olive oil, artefacts and wine for wheat with the Scythian princes who ruled the steppes and were buried with resplendent grave goods such as this gold comb. Greek influence is evident in the naturalistic style.

HOPLITES AND TYRANTS
700–550BC

Above: This 'Corinthian style' helmet, inscribed with the name Dendas, dates from c.500BC. Such helmets gave hoplites good head protection but limited visibility.

Below: The Chigi Vase (made in Corinth but found in central Italy, hence its name) is the earliest extant depiction of hoplites marching and fighting in formation. It dates from the 7th century BC, by which time the 'Hoplite Revolution' was well under way.

Although Homer's heroes had ridden to war in chariots for individual combat, in the post-Mycenaean age chariots were replaced by horsemen. As only rich aristocrats could afford armour and a horse, warfare remained dominated by noblemen. But by the 7th century BC growing wealth, in part fuelled by trade that provided cheaper metal, meant that more farmers of the middle class (in Athens called *zeugitae*, meaning owning a yoke of oxen) could afford armour and arms. This led to radical changes in warfare and in society.

THE HOPLITES' IMPORTANCE
The main battles of ancient Greece were decided by hoplites, heavy-armoured infantrymen. Fighting in close formation, with their long spears bristling in front of them, hoplites could outface cavalry and dominated warfare in Greece for almost 500 years. The oldest set of hoplite armour, unearthed near Argos, dates from c.700BC. It has a plumed helmet covering the head (helmets often covered the whole face, leaving mere slits for the eyes) and heavy metal cuirass covering the body. Most hoplites had metal grieves on their legs and all carried a large (about 1m/3ft in diameter) round shield on their left arm. In their right hand they carried a 3.5m/12ft spear. Each depended for protection on his open right flank on his neighbour. If one hoplite broke ranks and fled, the entire formation could be imperilled. To keep formation required practice. It also implied a novel equality between fighters: now the most blue-blooded aristocrat was equal on the battlefield to an unwashed farmer.

Hoplites made up about one-third of a typical Greek city's adult citizen population. (The majority of Greeks, who could not afford such full armour, were enrolled as light-armed troops, long considered of minor importance on or off the battle-field.) Marching and fighting together bred a new sense of camaraderie among

the hoplite class that had political and social effects. If fighting was no longer the preserve of nobles, soon politics too was seen as concerning far more of the people. As economic growth changed the Greek world, it increased the gap between the rich – who could import new luxuries – and the rest. Discontent with aristocratic rule, long taken for granted, increased. The nobles still monopolized power, but often treated politics as a frivolous if risky game between rival families, like the athletic contests they still dominated. But most Greeks wanted *eunomia* (good government), not *stasis* (the chaotic strife of aristocratic factions).

TYRANTS: NEW-STYLE RULERS
Quick to exploit such feelings were the men, often themselves rogue aristocrats, who seized power in many states as tyrants. (Greek *tyrannos* meant at first just unconstitutional ruler, boss or chief, not dictator in a modern sense.) From the mid-7th century BC tyrants appeared in cities that were often among the most dynamic in the Greek world. Typical was Corinth, a major trading city due to its position on the Isthmus, which produced fine pottery. Cypselus threw out its ruling Bacchiad family in 657BC, expelling other aristocrats and confiscating their property. Once in power, his regime proved so efficient and popular that he dispensed with a bodyguard. After he died in power in 625BC he was succeeded by his son Periander, who ruled for another 40 years.

Cypselus' example was soon followed in other cities such as nearby Megara and Sicyon. In neighbouring Argos the hereditary king Pheidon seems to have *become* a tyrant *c.*675BC, rebasing his rule on popular support. He reorganized the army as a hoplite force to crush the invading Spartans at Hysaia in 668BC. Tyrants, besides providing stable government, enriched their cities with temples and monuments. In Corinth, a dry shipway was built by Periander across the Isthmus, forerunner of the Corinth Canal.

Tyrannies spread across the Greek world from Sicily to Ionia. An unusually benevolent tyrant was Pittacus in Mytilene on the island of Lesbos, who resigned after ten years to general astonishment, the one tyrant to do so.

Among the Greek cities in Asia, tyranny was taken as the Greek norm by their Lydian and later by their Persian conquerors, who granted subject cities internal autonomy.

The last independent tyrant in eastern Greece was Polycrates of Samos, who built a famous temple, befriended the poet Anacreon and was *thalassocrat* (ruler of the seas) for a few years before being betrayed to the Persians and killed in 523BC. Few tyrant dynasties lasted long. At Corinth the tyranny collapsed soon after Periander's death. Tyranny was therefore a transitional phase for most Greek cities, with only unstable Sicilian cities reverting to tyranny in later years. And one supremely important state never experienced tyranny: Sparta.

Left: This vase from c.500BC shows hoplite warriors engaged in single combat. More typically, however, they fought in the disciplined ranks of the phalanx.

Below: A bronze helmet and cuirass, found near Argos and dating from the 7th century BC, are among the finest armour retrieved from the ancient world. Most hoplites would not have been able to afford anything so elaborate, instead having cuirasses of toughened linen.

THE IONIAN ENLIGHTENMENT
650–520BC

For the eastern Greeks of Ionia and the adjacent islands the period *c.*650–500BC saw an accelerating widening of horizons that was mental as much as physical. Their merchants, colonists and mercenaries explored the world from the Black Sea down to Egypt and as far east as Babylon (in modern Iraq), bringing home new ideas. This generated a novel vivacity that was different from the heroic age before and from the serious high Classical Age (480–322BC) that followed. Women at this time in Ionia probably enjoyed greater freedom than they did later (although this does not mean that they were remotely equal), while poets wrote more personally about life, love and death. The graceful Ionic column was developed at about this time, while Western philosophy and science were born together in the cities of Ionia. This time is called the Ionian Enlightenment.

Above: Sappho and Alcaeus were two of the greatest poets of the Lyric Age, writing intensely personal poems of love, death and loss as well as more convivial drinking songs and marriage epithalamia.

THE EGYPTIAN CONNECTION
Ionian nobles, including Alcaeus, were not above contacts with foreigners. Richest and strangest of foreign kingdoms was Egypt, from which came gold, ivory, wheat and papyrus, the best writing material. To preserve Egypt's independence, only recently regained from Assyrian domination, the pharaohs began hiring Greek hoplite mercenaries, already regarded as the world's best infantry. Some of these, employed in the far south of the country, left graffiti on the colossal statues of Abu Simbel that are still legible today. Greek merchants who penetrated into this enclosed, priest-ruled land were ultimately confined to one city, Naucratis in the Delta. Here Greeks from many different cities settled and traded, maintaining Hellenic customs in a very different world.

LYDIAN RULERS
Contacts with sophisticated peoples to the east first stimulated the Greeks, but the influence did not long remain one-way. In Anatolia the rich kingdom of Phrygia (its legendary king Midas' 'golden touch' suggests his immense wealth) was taken over by its neighbour Lydia in western Asia Minor *c.*680BC. Lydia's capital at Sardis was within easy reach of the coast, and Greek cities soon felt Lydian power encroaching on their cherished autonomy. Only Miletus, the largest and richest of the

Left: The expansion of Greek trade – north to the Black Sea, west to Italy and south to Egypt – opened Greek minds to richer, more sophisticated civilizations. It also made some Greeks much richer. Commerce was not at the time regarded as socially demeaning.

Right: Graffiti carved by Greek mercenaries in Egyptian service on the stones of Abu Simbel Temple in Upper Egypt indicate the fruitful interchange between Egyptian pharaohs and the Greeks in the 6th century BC. This special relationship ended with the Persian conquest of Egypt in 525BC.

Ionian cities, remained fully independent behind formidable walls. But the Lydian kings were generally benevolent rulers. They themselves came under such strong Greek influence that they were seen as philhellenes (supporters or admirers of things Greek).

Croesus, Lydia's most famous king, who came to the throne in 560BC, enriched the sanctuary at Delphi, holiest in the Greek world, employed Greek artists and helped to finance the vast Greek temple to Artemis (Diana) at Ephesus, later one of the Seven Wonders of the Ancient World. The Lydians traditionally introduced the first minted coins to the Greeks, who soon produced coins of great beauty themselves. Coinage further encouraged commerce, if widening the gap between rich and poor. Debts could now be computed, and wealth amassed, more easily. Above all, Lydia helped to shield the eastern Greeks from invading barbarians such as the Cimmerians, who ravaged Asia Minor in the 7th century, and from empires further east such as the Medes in Iran. At a battle in 585BC between Lydia and Media, an eclipse of the sun stopped the fighting. Both sides, awe-struck, agreed on the River Halys as a boundary.

PHILOSOPHY AND POETRY

This eclipse had been predicted by Thales, the first known Greek philosopher, who was also a scientist and was therefore interested in, rather than awed by, natural phenomena. A native of Miletus, he thought long and hard about what constituted ultimate reality. A school of philosophers followed him, called Milesian after Miletus. Thales' pupil Anaximander, who lived to c.536BC,

made the first map of the known world, realizing that the Earth hung unsupported in space though not that it was spherical. To show that philosophers could be practical, Thales reputedly diverted the River Halys to let King Croesus cross it.

The period also saw a flowering of a new form of poetry, not long heroic epics but short, personal lyric verses, often of poignant beauty. (*Lyric* meant 'sung to music of the lyre', a harp-like instrument.) The most famous are the love poems of Sappho of Lesbos *c*.600BC, many addressed to the girls whom she reputedly taught. Only fragments of her bitter-sweet poetry survive. More typical were the witty lyrics of Alcaeus, Anacreon and Archilochus. Archilochus wrote: "Some lucky Thracian has my fine shield, I had to run and dropped it in a wood. But I got clean away, thank God! So damn the shield, I'll get another just as good."

Society, while still aristocratic, grew more pleasure-loving and relaxed. *Symposia* (leisurely drinking parties with conversation and entertainment) became popular among the wealthier.

Below: The Tholos or Sanctuary of Athena Pronaia at Delphi was once the holiest sanctuary in the Greek world.

SPARTA: THE UNIQUE STATE
700–500BC

Above: Spartans attributed their unique constitution to Lycurgus, a semi-mythical figure who reputedly created Sparta's almost totalitarian regime after the city had suffered a major defeat.

Below: The Eurotas valley, in which Sparta sits, is the most fertile in southern Greece, giving Sparta rural wealth.

Sheltered by mountains, the valley of the Eurotas in Laconia in the south-east corner of the Peloponnese was half-isolated. The Spartans, a Dorian people who settled there *c.*1000BC, retained ancient Dorian customs, such as common messes for all male citizens and tribal education for children, that had been abandoned by other Dorians except those in even more remote Crete. But Spartans felt themselves to be different from other Greeks. They were surrounded by non-Dorian (but Greek) peoples in Laconia, whom they reduced to serfdom as *helots* (landbound slaves who provided food and produce for the ruling class, the *homoioi*), thereby gaining a valuable, if potentially dangerous, servile workforce.

By 700BC warfare had added the large, fertile territory of Messenia to the west, which was "good for ploughing and growing fruit", as the Spartan poet Tyrtaeus wrote. Despite being fellow Dorians, the Messenians were also enslaved. This conquest made Sparta the most powerful state in Greece. But it caused problems at home.

A RADICAL NEW CONSTITUTION

The wars had been won by Spartan hoplites, not aristocratic cavalry, but wealth was increasingly concentrated in the hands of a few. This caused discontent among ordinary Spartans struggling to maintain hoplites status. The resulting military weakness was shown up in defeat by Argos in 668BC and a revolt in Messenia. With Spartan power in danger of collapse, radical changes were needed.

Later, all reforms came to be attributed to Lycurgus, a semi-mythical figure, but the Delphic oracle, which Sparta regularly consulted, possibly played a part. Probably several individuals, including King Polydorus, were involved in helping to refound the state in the mid-7th century BC, giving it a constitution that was unusually complete and rigid. It was admired but not copied by other Greeks.

In theory, land was divided into equal lots owned inalienably by 9,000 *homoioi* (the elite ruling class, also known as 'Equals' and 'Spartiates'). They never worked their land but lived off the labour of the *helots*. The broad expanses of Messenia, reconquered by 640BC, gave Spartiates the landed wealth and leisure to train full time as soldiers. The Spartan army, distinguished by its scarlet cloaks and unbreakable discipline, became the one professional force in Greece, acknowledged as the best. In return for economic security, Spartiates surrendered their whole lives to the state.

DORIC DISCIPLINE

Every Spartan baby was examined by officials for deformities. Those considered unfit were exposed on a mountain. (Infanticide was practised in other Greek cities too but never so systematically.) At the age of seven, a boy was taken from his mother to begin his *agoge* (special training in a barracks). Wearing only a

thin tunic and no shoes, even in winter, he never had enough to eat, being expected to steal more food yet whipped if caught. At every stage he faced ferocious competition and punishments. Such training produced tough, obedient soldiers, taciturn – hence our word laconic (from Laconian) – dour and unimaginative.

At the age of 20 Spartiates had to win election to a mess, where they ate repellent meals, mostly 'Spartan black broth' (reputedly made from pork, blood, salt and vinegar). Homosexual affairs between prefects and younger boys were common. But Spartiates also had to produce children for the state after a strange marriage ceremony in which the bride's hair was shorn and she was dressed as a boy. Girls, too, exercised nearly naked, which shocked other Greeks.

Spartans were intensely pious, revering the gods, but they built few temples – Thucydides said that no one later seeing Sparta's sparse monuments would ever guess its power. Commerce was banned and there was no coinage, iron bars remaining the currency. Only *perioeci* ('dwellers around' in small towns who had to serve in the Lacadaemonian army), led normal lives. Every year 'war' was declared on the *helots*, during which potential rebels were secretly killed. Spartan art and poetry soon atrophied.

THE SPARTAN SYSTEM

Sparta strangely mixed oligarchy, democracy and monarchy. There were two kings – from the dynasties of the Agiads and

Eurypontids, both claiming descent from Hercules – who alone escaped the *agoge*. Only when leading the army abroad did they have real power. At home, they were constantly checked by the *ephors* (five officials chosen annually who wielded huge, if shadowy, power in this police state). The assembly consisted of all Spartans over the age of 30, who voted only on proposals put to it, one side shouting down the other – a method that Aristotle called childish but Jean-Jacques Rousseau later admired. There was also the *gerousia*, or senate, of men aged over 60 chosen for life.

Such a system was meant to defy all change, but some Spartiates finally became more equal than others. In the 4th century BC, as wealth from its newly gained empire flooded in, Lycurgus' system broke down. But by 550BC Sparta had forged a league of most states in the Peloponnese who were happy to follow it now that it seemed invincible.

Above: From the age of seven Spartan boys faced endless military-style drill. Toughness, conformity and unflinching obedience to orders were the aim, all individualism being stamped out.

Below: In its earlier days, before the grim regimentation of the Lycurgic system, Spartan potters produced fine vases such as this of Prometheus.

THE SPARTANS AND ALCOHOL

Despite worshipping many gods, the Spartans never worshipped Dionysus, the wine god. Also no *symposia*, the convivial drinking parties, were held in Spartan high society. Instead, young Spartiates were warned of the evils of alcohol by having *helots* paraded grotesquely drunk before them, to demonstrate the effects of inebriation.

Above: Olives, which grow extremely well in Greece, became the main crop of Attic agriculture after Solon prohibited the export of wheat.

ATHENS: REFORMERS AND TYRANTS 620–514 BC

In the 7th century BC Athens was a relative backwater. Although Attica, long united under Athens, was one of Greece's largest states, it lacked wide fertile valleys. It was still ruled by a clique of Eupatrid (hereditary noble) families, who controlled the Areopagus, the supreme council. But Athens was not immune to wider economic and social changes. In 632 BC Cylon, an aristocratic Olympic victor, seized the Acropolis, aiming to establish a tyranny. The *archon* (head official) Megacles – of the Eupatrid Alcmaeonid family, the most famous in Athenian history – tricked Cylon and his supporters out of the Acropolis and killed them. But the problems remained. Many poorer Athenians were *hektemoroi* (small farmers who owed their noble overlords a sixth of their produce). Falling into debt, they and their families might be enslaved and sold abroad, a fate that was even worse than a *helot*'s in Sparta.

In 625 BC the Eupatrid law giver Dracon drew up and published the first written law code. Athenians could now see how severe their laws actually were: someone could supposedly be executed for stealing a cabbage. (These laws were later called 'draconian'.) Popular discontent with the status quo grew until in 594 BC Solon, a Eupatrid but a noted critic of the rich, was given special powers. With them he launched a reform programme designed to avert tyranny by satisfying both the people and the rich.

"FREEING THE BLACK EARTH"
Solon's first measure was a "shaking off of debts". He stopped debt being secured on a person's liberty and freed all those already enslaved – he even tried to buy back Athenians sold abroad. He ordered the pulling up of stones that marked off land for aristocrats' tithes, "freeing the black earth" as he put it, and forbade the export of wheat from Attica to keep it cheap. Instead, he encouraged the export of olive oil; olive trees grow well in Attica, although they need 30 years to mature. Solon reformed the constitution, allowing all free citizens to attend the Assembly, which elected the *archons*. He established the Council of the 400, drawn by lot from the Assembly, as a preliminary debating body to balance the Areopagus. But he made both Eupatrids and rich commoners eligible for *archonship*

Right: The olive, mythical gift of the goddess Athena to her favoured city, is normally harvested in late winter or early spring. The trees take about 15–20 years to start bearing fruit and far longer to reach their prime. The olive-harvest was a popular topic for vase-painters, many of whose products were used to export the oil around the Mediterranean.

Right: The rapid growth of Athenian wealth and population under the Pisistratid 'tyrants' (meaning extra-constitutional rulers, not necessarily despots) in the 6th century BC led to a massive building programme. The huge Temple of Olympian Zeus proved too much even for the Pisitratid regime, however, and remained uncompleted for six centuries.

and so of the Areopagus, the highest court. Social divisions were now based on wealth not birth, allowing greater mobility. But Solon did not redistribute land as hoped or feared, for he was no revolutionary. "I gave the people such recognition as they deserved," he wrote, and went off on his travels. He left Athens more equitable if not democratic, for it was still led by aristocrats.

This was the problem. There were fierce divisions between the 'Coast' party of commercial interests and the 'Plain' of landowners, both led by irresponsible aristocrats. Years of bloody 'anarchy' – without elected *archons* – in the 580s saw war against next-door Megara go badly. Pisistratus, a noble who as *polemarch* (commander) had conquered Salamis island in 565BC, finally made himself tyrant in 561BC with other nobles' backing. They soon fell out and he was exiled. But he then made not one but two comebacks, the second time permanently in 546BC, supported by a third party of poorer farmers.

THE PISISTRATID REGIME

Once finally in power, Pisistratus surprised everyone by his moderation. Although some political rivals went into exile, there were no purges. Pisistratus helped Solon's reforms to take root by shielding the state from aristocratic faction. Unbullied by the rich, ordinary Athenians learnt to play a part in running their city. Pisistratus raised a tax of 10 per cent on farm produce, made loans on easy terms to help small farmers and started an economic boom, underpinned by stable government. To export Attic olive oil, superb new-style red figure vases

(on a black ground) were produced from 520BC onwards. Now Athenians became the finest of all Greek ceramicists. Athens also gained outposts on the Hellespont (Dardanelles), essential for protecting grain imports from the Black Sea. It still had only a tiny navy, however.

Athenian culture was not neglected either. Reputedly the first definitive edition of Homer's poems was compiled under Pisistratus' patronage, with ceremonial readings. He also inaugurated the Festival of the Great Dionysia, whose contests between different choruses later gave birth to Athenian tragedy and comedy. Among other monuments, he started a gigantic temple to Zeus, king of the gods, not completed for six centuries. When Pisistratus' sons Hippias and Hipparchus jointly succeeded their father at his death in 527BC and continued his policies, theirs must have seemed the most stable regime after Sparta's in Greece. But it was not to last.

Below: One of the 'Seven Sages of Greece', Solon, reformed the Athenian constitution, trying to avert social revolution or tyranny – unsuccessfully with regard to the latter.

ATHENS: THE DEMOCRATIC REVOLUTION 514–490BC

The trigger for the downfall of the Pisistratids was a quarrel over a boy's affections (very Greek, some might think), but the real causes went much deeper. By 514BC many states considered tyrants to be oppressive and turned for help to Sparta, which generally disliked tyrants as upstarts. When Harmodius and Aristogeiton, who were later hailed as liberators and had fine statues erected in their memory, killed Hipparchus for personal reasons in 514BC, the surviving Pisistratid, Hippias, became paranoid. Retreating to the Acropolis, he started a truly tyrannical reign of terror that brought about his own downfall.

THE ROLE OF CLEISTHENES

Cleisthenes, head of the Athenian Alcmaeonid family but currently in exile, had been wooing the Delphic oracle with gifts. Whenever Sparta consulted the oracle, it now replied: "Free Athens!" Finally, in 510BC a Spartan army under King Cleomones marched into Attica, and Hippias, with his supporters, fled to the Persians. Cleomones, like most Athenian nobles, then expected a return to the good old days of noble-led factions with the people merely acting as supporters. But Athens had changed. It was the genius of Cleisthenes to realize and take advantage of this.

After losing the election for the *archonship* in 508BC to Isagoras, who had Cleomones' backing, in 507BC Cleisthenes proposed a radical reordering of the whole state. In future the Assembly of all citizens voting together would be completely sovereign, and a new Council of 500, chosen by lot from all citizens irrespective of wealth, would act as a *probouletic* (preliminary debating) body. Cleisthenes abolished the old Ionic 'tribes' and replaced them with ten new ones, all artificial despite being named after ancient heroes. Each new tribe had three electoral wards called *trittyes* (thirds).

Above: The bright colours and alert energy of this koure *(young girl) embody Athens' optimistic energy at the dawn of democracy in the late 6th century* BC.

Right: The 'Treasury of the Athenians' at Delphi, lavishly built all in marble, was probably erected in the 490s BC by the young democracy in gratitude to Apollo's oracle, whose utterances "Free Athens!" had so aided the city.

"THE FINEST FIGHTERS IN THE WORLD"

"So Athens went from strength to strength and proved, if proof is needed, how noble a thing freedom is, for while oppressed they had no more success in war than their neighbours. But once they were free, they proved the finest fighters in the world," wrote the historian Herodotus admiringly. With the spoils of victory the Athenians raised a huge bronze statue of a chariot drawn by four horses, prominently visible near the Propylae on the Acropolis, to celebrate their new democracy.

These 30 *trittyes* contained *demes* from all three old rival factions: the city and its environs, the coastal lands and the uplands. Every citizen had to register afresh in a *deme*, which was administered by a locally elected *demarch*, and was then allocated to a *trittyes* and so to a tribe. This vastly reduced the influence of local squires on elections.

Unsurprisingly, Isagoras and his aristocratic supporters were horrified. They called on Cleomones, who had no time at all for such dangerous democratic ideas and marched straight back to Athens. There he exiled 700 Alcmaeonid supporters – Cleisthenes had already wisely withdrawn – re-established the old regime and then retired with Isagoras to the Acropolis for a celebratory dinner. But while they were celebrating, the noise of a popular rising in the streets below first amazed and then alarmed them. Although lacking any proper nobles to lead them, the people of Athens had risen in revolt on their own – an unprecedented event. Soon, surrounded and without provisions, the Spartans and Isagoras had to surrender ignominiously and leave Athens.

Cleisthenes now returned in triumph, and his reforms were implemented. He probably at this time added some immigrants from Ionia, long resident in the city, to the citizen list. As a safety valve, to stop any individual growing too powerful, he also introduced a novel scheme: ostracism. Every year there would be a vote on whether to hold an ostracism. If 6,000 citizens wanted to, they would inscribe names of men to be ostracized on bits of pottery (*ostrakia*). The man most frequently named had to go into exile for ten years but did not lose his citizenship or property. Cleisthenes, whether or not he had intended to, had created the first full democracy in Greece, probably in the whole world.

DEMOCRACY TRIUMPHANT

The new democracy in Athens was soon to be put to the test. Cleomones, burning for revenge, summoned the armies of Sparta and her Peloponnesian allies, much the most formidable force in Greece, to invade Attica, while the Thebans and Chalcians, Athens' old enemies, attacked from the north-east. The Athenians were undaunted and marched out to Eleusis to meet the Spartan-led army – which promptly turned back. The Corinthians, a major contingent of the army, had changed their minds, while the other Spartan king, Demaratus, for reasons unknown, also went home, forcing Cleomones to follow suit. The Athenians then swung east to defeat the Thebans before crossing to Euboea, where they routed the Chalcians. They subsequently settled 4,000 colonists on Chalcian land.

Below: Harmodius and Aristogeiton are shown here as the heroic liberators who killed the tyrant Hipparchus in 514BC. Although only a Roman copy of the second pair of original Greek bronzes – which were made in the 470s BC, the first pair having been carried off by the Persians in 480BC – the original group's dynamic strength shines through. It typified Athenian democracy's abounding new self-confidence.

COUNTDOWN TO WAR
488–481BC

Above: View of Mount Athos in northern Greece, off whose rocky shore Mardonius was once shipwrecked in a storm.

Below: Persia's lengthy preparations for the grand invasion of 480BC included cutting a canal through the flat peninsula north of Mt Athos shown below. This was intended both to protect the invasion fleet from storms that had wrecked earlier ships and to overawe the Greeks.

For ordinary Athenians victory at Marathon appeared to lift the threat of Persian invasion for good. But they were wrong. The Great King was only marginally harmed by what was to him a peripheral battle. It needed to be avenged, of course, but the Persian Empire was still expanding and the conquest of Greece – an invitingly divided if troublesome land – remained on the agenda. This time, however, the Achaemenid Empire would act like the superpower it was. Overwhelming force on land and sea would be gathered to shock and awe Greece into submission.

PREPARATIONS FOR WAR

Mardonius, a noted young Persian general, had earlier been shipwrecked in a storm off Mt Athos in northern Greece, so it was decided to dig a canal through the Athos peninsula's neck to avoid this recurring. Thousands of conscripted workers took three years to dig a canal deep enough for galleys, while a pontoon bridge was built over the Hellespont (Dardanelles) to let the invading army cross speedily. Destroyed by storms, it was hastily rebuilt. Supplies were stockpiled in forts along the Aegean north coast and the River Strymon in Macedonia bridged. The death of Darius in late 486BC interrupted preparations only briefly. The throne passed smoothly to Xerxes his son (and Cyrus' grandson) and a revolt in Egypt was suppressed. Finally, in April 481BC, the Great King left Susa – a date marked by a solar eclipse – and slowly marched west with imposing majesty.

Forces had been levied from across his huge empire, from Africa to India. Some were not experienced fighters but many, such as the Persian cavalry, Saka mounted archers, fishmail-armoured Medes and the 10,000 Immortals (royal guards), were. The fleet, too, was mostly professional, its 300 Phoenician galleys being thought the best afloat. Herodotus, seldom reliable on figures, totals the Persian forces at 1.7 million – an absurd figure, such a horde being impossible to feed. Modern estimates suggest *c.*250,000 soldiers, supported by a fleet of *c.*600 warships.

To deny Greece help from its Western compatriots, Carthage was urged to attack Greek Sicily. Meanwhile, Persian gold subverted north Greece. Macedonia was already a client state; Thessaly, due south, seemed ready to 'medize', its nobility favouring Persia. Beyond, central Greece looked open to pressure, while many Aegean islands were Persian-controlled. The stage was set.

THE GROWTH OF DEMOCRACY

Back in Athens, at first it was politics as usual. Celebrated for his Marathon victory, Miltiades led an attack on Paros

Left: The trireme, with 170 rowers (all free citizens) and 30 marines, was the backbone of the Athenian fleet by 480BC. Although such ships certainly had three tiers of oars, how they really worked has never been established. The Olympias, a recreation launched in 1987, moved only slowly, soon exhausting even its youthful crew.

Above: The years leading up to the Persian invasion of 480BC saw the emergence of full democracy in Athens and, not by coincidence, of classical naturalism in the arts, exemplified by the 'Critias Boy' of c.482BC.

in 489BC. He failed abysmally, was prosecuted, heavily fined and died in debt. After 487BC election to the *archonship* was replaced by sortition (lottery). This reduced the powers of the *polemarch* (military *archon*), for a randomly chosen leader might lack military experience. Instead, the ten *strategoi* (generals) elected from each tribe became the real commanders. This marked a further advance in democracy: anyone, not just the rich, could be elected *strategos*. Ostracism was now used, probably for the first time. Among those ostracized were Pisistratids and Alcmaeonid aristocrats. The young democracy was flexing its muscles.

THE BIRTH OF ATHENS' NAVY

Athens remained mainly a land power, proud of its hoplites' victory at Marathon. One man, however, saw danger in this. Themistocles, a stocky, energetic man, brilliant at courting the people, was a radical democrat though aristocratic himself, at least on his father's side. Elected *archon* in 493BC, he began in the 480s to press for a huge expansion of the navy. This was unpopular with the rich, who would have to pay for it, while small farmers saw no need for it. When in

483BC a huge new lode of silver was found at the mines of Laurium, a great debate began in Athens about how to spend it. Aristides, now the conservative leader (nicknamed 'the Just' because he famously took no bribes), suggested distributing the windfall among the citizens, an idea with obvious appeal.

But Themistocles urged that it all be spent on a massive new navy of triremes, the triple-tiered galleys that now dominated sea war. As a Persian threat still seemed remote, Themistocles pointed instead to the island of Aegina visible across the water, whose ships raided Attic coasts with impunity. His eloquence finally carried the day.

A crash programme was begun that within three years gave Athens the largest navy in Greece: 200 triremes, each requiring a crew of 170 citizen rowers and 30 sailors and marines. This vast new force – which committed ordinary Athenians to learn to fight at sea, sweating at their oars rather than parading proudly on land – was built and trained within three years. Just in time, it turned out. Meanwhile Aristides was ostracized, Athenians sickening of hearing him forever called 'the Just'.

THERMOPYLAE: LEONIDAS AND 'THE 300' 480BC

Above: In Persia's grand army of c.250,000 men – the largest force yet assembled – were tens of thousands of archers. They fired so many arrows at the Spartans at Thermopylae that the Greeks joked at being able to fight in the shade.

In late 481BC news of the huge army being assembled at Sardis reached the Greeks, its numbers amplified by the Persians, masters of psychological warfare. Persian envoys again went around Greece demanding submission. Most cities prevaricated. Athens and Sparta called a Panhellenic League at the Corinth Isthmus, to which 40 states sent envoys. Many did not. Swallowing its pride, Athens accepted Spartan leadership on land *and* sea, despite providing most of the fleet. The League warned possible 'medizers' that their lands would be 'tithed to Apollo', i.e. taken from them, if they collaborated.

THE ORACLE'S PROPHECY
But Greeks were hardly encouraged to resist by the Delphic oracle's doom-laden prophecies. "Fly far, far away; Leave home, town and castle and do not stay," it told the Athenians. When they asked again, they were told to trust in the "wooden walls" but warned: "Divine Salamis will destroy the children of women." This perplexed the Athenian Assembly, some taking "wooden walls" to mean those once surrounding the Acropolis, others their new fleet. Themistocles, now Athens' effective leader, favoured the latter, and his advice was accepted: if necessary, the Athenians would evacuate their entire city and take to the sea. Their decision saved Greece.

DEFENCE POSITIONS
In June, when some Thessalians suggested holding the pass at Tempe beneath Mt Olympus, 10,000 hoplites went north. They had to return hastily, for Persian forces found other undefended passes. The next possible line was in central Greece, where the mountains almost touched the sea at Thermopylae. A fleet based at Artemisium in west Euboea could support an army there. King Leonidas, with an elite of 300 older Spartiates ("all with living sons") set out, collecting allied troops en route until 7,000 hoplites manned an old wall at Thermopylae. Meanwhile, 200 triremes sailed north to Artemisium. There they awaited the Persian colossus.

This took its time, advancing in slow splendour, "drinking rivers dry" as June passed into July. From Delphi came a cryptic last message: "Pray to the winds!" Greeks knew that, as summer advanced,

Left: As news of Persian invasion plans reached the Greeks in late 481BC, a pan-hellenic Congress was called at Corinth, the wealthy city controlling the Isthmus. There 40 cities agreed plans that gave the Spartans overall command at land and sea and threatened retribution for any state that 'medized' (collaborated with the Persians).

sudden storms could arise in the Aegean, knowledge the Persians lacked. Leonidas was not on a suicide mission, although the Delphic oracle had prophesied Sparta's fall unless one of its kings died. He hoped to hold the Persians long enough for the main Spartan army, due to celebrate the Carnaean and Olympic festivals in August, to march north. Thermopylae was a splendid position provided it was not outflanked by sea or by land. But there were paths over the mountains, known to locals.

In August, the ground shaking beneath their feet, the Persians finally arrived. So did the winds, gales scattering both Greek and Persian fleets. Xerxes, who could not let his huge army stand still for long or it would starve, ordered a direct assault on the Greeks by heavy infantry – Medes used to mountain warfare. They were not, however, used to Spartiates in their killing prime and made no progress against the hoplite wall. Then the elite Immortals joined the battle, to be repelled also.

THE BATTLE OF THERMOPYLAE
At sea things were more equal, both fleets reassembling, only battered. But a Persian force, sent to outflank the Greeks

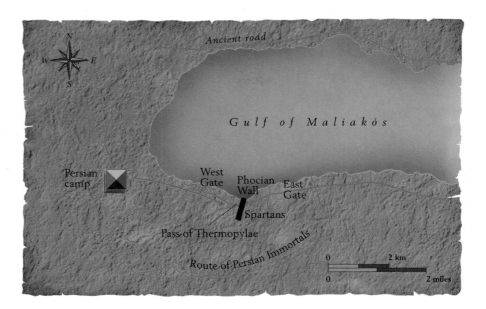

Above: The narrow pass at Thermopylae, where the mountains then nearly touched the sea, provided the best defensive position in Greece. Sparta's king Leonidas, with an advance army of 7,000 men (including 300 Spartiates) marched north to hold it. But a mountain path allowed the Persians finally to circumvent the Greeks.

Below: This statue of a Spartan warrior – possibly even a portrait of King Leonidas himself – reveals the disciplined determination that made Spartans the best soldiers in Greece.

DELPHI'S AMBIGUOUS ROLE
The Delphic oracle, sacred to Apollo, was the most revered in Greece. Its site, stunningly beautiful, was called *omphalos* (navel of the world). There the Greeks dedicated many of their finest shrines and offerings. Its Pythean priestess gave famously obscure replies to questions, so preserving its reputation for infallibility. But Delphi's role in the great Persian wars was so inglorious that it could be suspected almost of 'medizing'. In 480BC Persian power appeared overwhelming to the shrewd priests, and Greece's chance of victory looked poor. The Delphic priests were realists: better to maintain a diplomatic neutrality than openly support either side.

by sailing down Euboea's east coast, was wrecked, removing a major threat. The running naval battle that followed in the straits off Artemisium saw the Greeks, though outnumbered, undefeated. Then catastrophic news from Thermopylae changed everything.

Persian gold had found a local traitor, Ephialtes, to guide them over a mountain path to behind the wall. The Immortals followed him on a night march up to a pass where some Phocians, stationed as guards, panicked, withdrawing to let the Persians descend.

Leonidas had just enough warning to send off most troops before being surrounded. Then, with his Spartiates, some unwilling Thebans and dogged Thespians, probably about 1,500 men in all, he took his last stand. This was bloody and desperate, the Spartans fighting with bare hands after their swords and spears had splintered, until finally all lay dead around the corpse of their king. The road to Athens lay open.

SALAMIS: VICTORY AT SEA
480BC

Above: The island of Aegina, with its fine temple to Apheia, sheltered many Athenian refugees forced to evacuate their city.

Below: Themistocles, the Athenian leader, realizing that the Greek fleet lacked the skill and numbers to win a battle in open waters, tricked the Persians into sending their fleet into the narrows between Salamis island and the mainland. There the Greeks' heavier but inexperienced galleys crowded the Persians together so that they could not move, and so won decisively.

Days after Thermopylae, Themistocles reached Piraeus with the battle-scarred Greek fleet. It had slipped away by night after hearing of Leonidas' end. He now oversaw the evacuation of Athens. Women and children trundled possessions down to embark for Aegina, Troezen (which offered to educate all Athens' children) and Salamis. This small island became the Panhellenic League's head-quarters and the tented city of Athens-in-exile. Not everything could be taken – one dog swum loyally after his master's boat, dying as he reached land. Nor would every Athenian leave. Some diehards retreated to the Acropolis behind wooden barricades. After firing the barricades, the Persians captured the citadel. They killed everyone there, including priests and priestesses, burning the temples – an act of sacrilegious terror never forgotten. They looted the main city while the Great King deliberated.

A NAVAL WAITING GAME
At Salamis there was disagreement among the Greeks. Some Peloponnesians, alarmed as the Persian fleet neared Salamis, wanted to retreat to the Isthmus, where a wall had been built. This option, which abandoned all hope of regaining Athens quickly, was rejected by Themistocles. He also realized that the Greek fleet, outnumbered and less skilled than the Persian, must not fight in open waters. Battle at Artemisium had shown that only at close quarters could Greeks hope to defeat Persians. It was necessary to be bottled up at Salamis, as the other Greek leaders finally accepted. A waiting game followed, but neither side could afford to wait for too long.

Persia had problems too. It had lost so many ships – through storms and enemy action – that it no longer had over-whelming naval superiority. The Greeks had about 300 seaworthy triremes by this time, the Persians probably only around 100 more. Persia could not afford to divide its fleet again, as it had before Artemisium, to threaten the Peloponnese simultaneously. Also, it was already mid-September. The campaigning season would not last much longer before autumnal storms began.

GREEK TRICKERY
Xerxes was therefore delighted when a secret messenger arrived from Themistocles, claiming his master was really the king's friend. The Greeks, he announced, were divided – the Persians must have found this credible – with many planning to flee. All the Persians had to do was to send ships to the straits' exits to catch the Greek triremes sailing off at dawn. (Sails were stowed away while fighting.) Xerxes gave his orders: Egyptian galleys would guard the western exit while the main fleet, of Phoenicians, Ionians and Carians, would enter the eastern straits to seize the fleeing Greeks. He himself would oversee his forces from a throne on the shore.

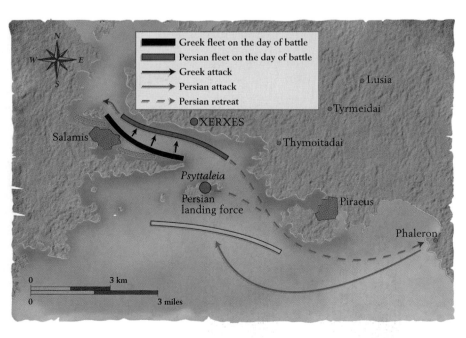

That fateful night, probably the 19/20 September, Persia's ships sailed to their appointed stations.

THE BATTLE OF SALAMIS

However, Themistocles' message was a hoax designed to lure the Persians into the Salamis straits, less than 1.6km/1 mile wide. According to Herodotus, only Themistocles knew of this. But the overall plan must have been widely discussed and agreed earlier, for the Greeks reacted swiftly to news of the Persian advance brought by Aristides. (All Athenian exiles had been recalled.)

As the sun rose over Salamis, the Persian ships nosed forward under their royal master's eye: Phoenicians on the right closest to the mainland, Carians and Cilicians in the centre, Ionians on the left. Facing them were Athenian ships on the Greek left, seemingly recoiling in fear, Peloponnesians in the centre and Aeginetans on the right. Xerxes saw far-off Corinthian ships hoisting sail and appearing to flee westward, as he had been told. All seemed to be going to plan.

Suddenly the Athenians stopped backing to surge forward, singing a *paean* (hymn). The Phoenician flagship, commanded by a brother of Xerxes, was attacked first, its royal admiral killed as he boarded an Athenian trireme. Soon the heavier Greek galleys were smashing into Persians ships too tight-packed to manoeuvre or even row properly. Some of the Persian fleet beached their crippled ships on the mainland. Several Phoenician captains were summarily executed by Xerxes for cowardice. Queen Artemisia of Halicarnassus, a Persian vassal, won his praise for apparently sinking a Greek ship, but this was actually a Persian galley blocking her escape. The Corinthians now returned to join the battle while the Egyptian squadron still waited idly.

By the afternoon the Greeks had won a crushing victory: only 40 of their own ships sunk for 200 of the Persians, the Phoenicians suffering especially. Persian power had experienced its first momentous defeat. King Xerxes returned ignominiously but safely by the same road to Asia. He left behind his unbeaten and large professional army, and much of Greece still in Persian hands.

Above: A 19th-century artist's colourful vision of the Greek fleet re-entering the Piraeus, the port of Athens, in triumph after the Battle of Salamis.

Below: King Xerxes ordered the building of a pontoon bridge over the Hellespont (Dardanelles) to allow the immense Persian army to cross from Asia to Europe early in 480BC. Jean Adrien Guignet's 19th-century painting shows Xerxes at the Hellespont.

PLATAEA: VICTORY ON LAND 479BC

Above: A statuette from the 6th century BC showing a typically tough Spartan hoplite soldier, the victor of Plataea.

The Athens to which its citizens returned that autumn was a gutted, half-ruined city. There was little comfort there. Nor were the Persians safely distant. The Persian general Mardonius, allowed to cherry pick an army for his command in Greece, had chosen the best – Persian and Median heavy cavalry, Sakae mounted archers – before settling in Thessaly for the winter. There began a war of words and nerves. Paradoxically, the Athenians, whose navy had effectively won the war at sea, now needed the Peloponnesians to fight a land battle in Boeotia to prevent Persia re-invading Attica.

AN OFFER OF PEACE...

The Spartans, with the immediate threat to the Peloponnese removed, were again loath to commit themselves, being worried about Argos, their old enemy close to home. Further arguments at League headquarters in Corinth produced no agreement, although when Themistocles visited Sparta he was fêted as a hero. This did him little good in Athens, where his opponents, the formerly ostracized Aristides and Xanthippus, were elected *strategoi* (generals) for 479BC. To Athens that spring came Alexander I of Macedonia, a wily monarch who had involuntarily entertained the Great King earlier. The offer he brought to the Athenians amid the rubble of their wrecked Agora sounded tempting: the Great King would, if Athens changed sides, not only forgive all of Athens' past acts against him but grant it special self-governing status, like Tyre or Sidon, money to restore her temples and support against her enemies. "Why be so mad as to resist the King?" asked Alexander. "You can never beat him and cannot hold out forever."

... REJECTED

The Athenians responded magnificently: "We know well enough that Persian power is many times greater than ours... But we want above all to be free, so we will never surrender... Tell Mardonius that the Athenians say: 'While the sun takes his normal path, we will make no agreement with Xerxes, but will defend ourselves, trusting in the gods and heroes who fight for us and whose temples he has burnt'." With this Alexander was dismissed. In June, Mardonius swept south again into Attica, and Athenians evacuated their city for the second time in ten months. Their envoys in Sparta warned that they might be forced to accept Mardonius' peace offers after all.

Left: After their victories, the Greeks liked to portray their opponents as unmanly cowards. This vase shows a Persian almost running away. In fact Persians were fine soldiers, despite defeats on land and sea in 480/79BC, but Greek hoplites made far better infantry than their Persian counterparts, as Plataea showed.

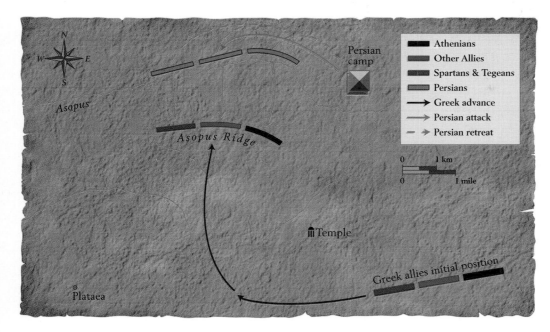

Left: The Persian army under Mardonius met the massed Greek hoplite forces in 479BC in a plain near Plataea in central Greece for the deciding land battle. When the Greeks began moving from their hilltop positions, Mardonius attacked their exposed flanks. But the disciplined Spartan phalanx routed the Persians.

Suddenly, Sparta's *ephors* announced that their army was already on the march with its allies. Mardonius, on hearing the news, torched all Athens before withdrawing to Boeotia, good country for horsemen.

PLATAEA: THE SPARTAN VICTORY

Mardonius' army numbered 60–70,000, judging by the size of the fortified camp he built near Thebes. In contrast, Aristides led 8,000 Athenian hoplites to join the League forces at Eleusis under the command of the Spartan regent Pausanias. (One Spartan king was still a boy, the other was Leotychides, commanding the fleet.) There they swore the Oath of Plataea, which began: "I will fight to the death and will not count my life more precious than freedom." It marked the high point of Greek unity. Then the hoplite army of *c*.40,000 men, the largest yet assembled, crossed into Boeotia. It took up a position on the slopes of Mt Cithaeron above the River Asopus.

There both sides waited, for Pausanias would not descend into a plain favourable to cavalry, while Mardonius would not attack uphill against hoplites. Mardonius finally sent mounted archers under Masistius, a famed nobleman, to make the Greek hoplites break rank. But Masistius was himself killed, his death grieving the Persians. The Greeks were less well supplied with food and water than the Persians, however, especially after their main spring had been destroyed, and so Pausanias decided to move the Greek army east toward Plataea, on to the low Asopus ridge, to improve water supplies. They began moving by night – a difficult manoeuvre that found many not in their new posts at dawn.

Mardonius, seeing the Greeks in such confusion, ordered an attack on the Spartans and their Tegean allies: *c*.11,000 men cut off from the main army. While Theban hoplites attacked the separated Athenians, Persian archers hailed arrows at the Spartans, killing many men. Yet Pausanias would not give the order to charge until the omens from sacrifices predicted victory. When they finally did, the Spartans rolled forwards, their disciplined phalanx carving a way through the Persians. After Mardonius, conspicuous on his white horse, was killed, his troops broke and fled toward their fort. But this proved to be no refuge, as the Athenians stormed it, killing all inside.

This battle marked the end of the Persian invasion. On the same day traditionally, the Greek fleet across the Aegean defeated the Persian fleet at Mycale (a naval battle fought on land), to which the Persians had retreated. This completed the Greeks' triumph.

Below: Spartan hoplites such as this soldier proved superior to the Persians at Plataea, the greatest land battle yet fought in Greece.

VICTORY IN THE WEST
480–474 BC

Above: Coins such as this, showing a triumphant charioteer and a winged nike *(victory), were struck to celebrate victories such as Gelon's defeat of Carthage at Himera in 480 BC.*

Above: The Greeks produced the world's first really beautiful coins, often to celebrate victories. This fine piece commemorates the Syracusan victory over the Carthaginians in 480 BC.

Right: Greek colonies spread throughout all Sicily except the north-west, where the Carthaginians maintained some fortified trading posts. The island's fertile interior remained inhabited mostly by native Sicels, who only slowly became Hellenized.

Before 500 BC, Carthaginian and west Greek colonies had only occasionally fought each other. The Carthaginians, who were primarily merchants, established what were really large fortified trading posts, while the Greek colonies often became rich trading and farming cities. Carthage had prevented Greek colonization of southern Spain, Corsica and Sardinia, but in Sicily it had only three small cities in the north-west around Palermo. By contrast, Greek cities lined Sicily's south, east and north-east coasts.

Tyrants were a common form of government in western Greek cities around 500 BC, gaining power easily amid the recurrent political crises. Gelon, already tyrant of Gela, seized Syracuse in 485 BC and made it capital of what became Sicily's most powerful state. He forcibly moved to Syracuse the luckless populations of Gela and other nearby cities. Linked by marriage to Theron, tyrant of Acragas (Agrigento), the second largest Greek city in Sicily, Gelon treated his poorer citizens badly, enfranchizing only the rich. His power lay in his many mercenaries, whom he made citizens of Syracuse. But his fleet of 200 triremes and army of 20,000 hoplites made him formidable, and in 481 BC the Panhellenic League begged for his assistance against Persia. In return, he demanded leadership of the League either by land or sea, both unacceptable to Sparta. As it turned out, Gelon had pressing problems close to home and gave no help to the League.

CARTHAGINIAN EXPANSION
The Persians, probably using the Phoenicians as intermediaries, had urged Carthage to distract the western Greeks.

IN PRAISE OF TYRANNY
Pindar and Bacchylides, among the greatest poets of the 5th century BC, hymned the achievements of the tyrants Gelon and Hieron, their poems dwelling on the luxurious splendours of both their courts. Hieron also made lavish offerings to the Greek shrines at Olympia and Delphi, the most famous probably being the superb bronze charioteer of c.470 BC.

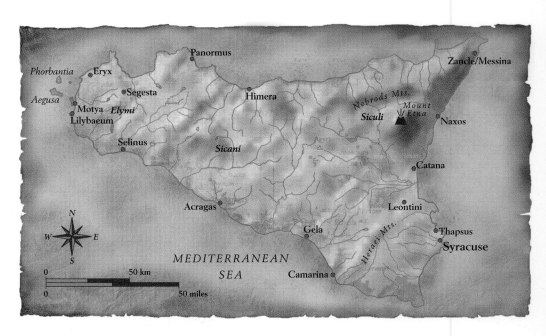

Divisions among the Greeks now gave Carthage, already larger and richer than any other city in the Mediterranean, an opportunity to gain control of all Sicily. Theron of Acragas had just expelled Terillus, ruler of Himera, a Greek city on the north coast. Terillus appealed to the Greek tyrant of Rhegium (Reggio), who in turn asked Carthage for help. With this excuse, an armada that must have been long prepared sailed from Carthage. It was reportedly 300,000 strong, with Carthaginian infantry plus Libyan, Iberian, Sardinian and Ligurian mercenaries, transported in 3,000 ships and guarded by 200 galleys. Only the last figure seems credible, but it was certainly a huge force meant, like its Persian equivalent, to overawe the Greeks.

THE SIEGE OF HIMERA

Hamilcar, the Carthaginian *shophet* (commander), embarked this army and sailed for Palermo, where he landed only after losing most of his horse-transports in storms – a loss that was to prove crucial. He then marched on Himera and besieged it, building a fortified camp by the sea and another one inland for his vast army. Theron, reaching Himera just ahead of the Carthaginians, ordered its gates to be walled up (to prevent surrender as well as to keep out the enemy) and sent urgent messages to Syracuse. Gelon, who had been waiting, marched with 50,000 men to join forces with the Himerans, who reopened their gates.

Both sides then waited – showing that the Carthaginians lacked overwhelming superiority – until Gelon had a stroke of luck. Hamilcar had asked Selinus, a half-Greek Sicilian ally, to send him some cavalry. Their reply fell into Gelon's hands, and Syracusan cavalry entered the Carthaginian camp disguised as Selinans. Then they attacked the Carthaginians from the rear.

The battle that followed was confused and bloody. The Syracusan infiltrators killed Hamilcar as he was sacrificing to the gods (in one story he immolated himself on a pyre), but the battle was nearly lost when many Greeks stopped to plunder the Carthaginian camp. Final victory was total, however, with few Carthaginians returning home. Instead, many mercenaries ended their lives as slaves, building grand temples for the Greek cities, especially in Acragas' Vale of Temples. But the Carthaginian colonies in north-west Sicily were left alone.

A TIME OF PEACE AND PLENTY

The following decades were prosperous ones for Greek Sicily. Hieron peacefully succeeded his brother Gelon as ruler of Syracuse in 478BC. He won a great naval victory four years later when the Etruscans, still expanding their power in central Italy, were defeated at Cumae (Cyme) in 474BC. This marked the end of Etruscan expansion as definitively as Himera and the east Greek victories had checked Carthaginian and Persian power.

After 460BC democracy replaced tyranny in most major Sicilian cities. They then enjoyed a long period of unusual domestic accord and foreign peace in what came to be seen as Sicily's golden age, marked by splendid temple-building at Acragas and other cities.

Above: The Valley of the Temples at Agrigento in Sicily is one of the world's most important archaeological sites.

Below: Syracuse became the richest and most powerful Greek city in Sicily, spreading up the hills from the original island colony of Ortygia. The fortifications at Euryalus high above were to prove crucial to its defence.

CHAPTER III

ATHENS AT ITS ZENITH

478–431BC

Between its triumph in the Persian Wars in 479BC and the Peloponnesian War that began in 431BC, Athens enjoyed a golden half-century, becoming the greatest of all Greek cities. Although the era ended in political and military disasters, these do not diminish Athens' achievements, as classical culture and full democracy came of age. When Pericles, the democratic statesman, claimed that Athens was 'the educator of Greece', he was not bragging. Athens demonstrated that democracy, in its deepest (if not widest) sense, could encourage intellectual and cultural excellence: not dumbing down but climbing up. In drama, art, philosophy, architecture and politics it was a brilliant age.

Classical Athens had its downsides. Its brilliance came partly from ruling and taxing its supposed allies; full enjoyment of democracy was denied to women, foreign residents and slaves; and Athens could behave brutally toward its enemies. Athenians, intoxicated by their city's primacy, often displayed an arrogance that finally united many other Greeks against them. Despite such faults, Athens incarnated so much of what is noblest about ancient Greece that we still see it mainly through Athenian eyes. Even other Greeks acknowledged this quality. Pindar of Thebes, a city often hostile to Athens, wrote: "O shining city, violet-crowned and famous in song/Bastion of Hellas, glorious Athens, city of godlike men".

Left: The Parthenon, built between 447BC and 432BC, embodies Athenian genius at its most radiant.

SPARTAN FAILINGS, ATHENIAN INITIATIVE 479–478BC

Above: The Parthenon in Athens, set high on the Acropolis. Without its city walls, Athens was very vulnerable to attack.

Below: Under the guidance of Themistocles, one of Athens' greatest democratic statesmen, the city hastily rewalled itself after the wars, now incorporating the Diplyon and Kerameikos areas.

After the defeats of the Persian army at Plataea and the Persian fleet at Mycale in Ionia in 479BC, many Greek islands and cities in Asia happily threw off their Persian allegiance. This meant that the Panhellenic League had to decide how to defend the eastern Greeks against Persia. The Spartans suggested moving their populations to Greece proper, where they could have the territory of cities that had 'medized' (collaborated with Persia). After this impractical plan was vetoed, the League decided to continue the war against Persia, which still controlled many strongholds in the north and east Aegean.

The League's fleet sailed north to the Hellespont in the summer of 479BC, where they found that Xerxes' grandiose pontoon bridge linking Europe and Asia had been demolished. The Peloponnesians, reassured that the Persians could not easily reinvade, now sailed home. But Xanthippus, the Athenian *strategos*, led the Athenian and Ionian ships to attack Sestos on the Hellespont. This was no easy task, as it turned out, for

GREEKS AND BARBARIANS

Greeks called all non-Greek peoples *barbaros*, from which comes our word barbarian. This did not originally mean barbaric – uncouth, uncivilized – in the modern sense, for it applied equally to peoples such as the Persians, Phoenicians and Egyptians, who were generally more sophisticated than the Greeks. It just meant people who spoke another language that, to Greeks, sounded like 'bar-bar'. But after the Persian Wars, Greeks began to feel psychologically and morally superior to 'the barbarians who dwell in Asia', in other words within Persia's vast empire. Greeks alone enjoyed freedom, not having to grovel before a despot. Of course, there were plenty of tyrannies in Greece, and Athens or Sparta could behave despotically towards other cities, but this did not upset the Greek view of the world as divided into two: Greeks, free and independent; and barbarians, perhaps rich, often decadent, but always servile. Aeschylus' play *The Persians*, first produced in 472BC, exemplifies this attitude.

its Persian governor held on for months. But by winter Sestos fell and Xanthippus could return triumphant to Athens.

REFORTIFYING ATHENS

Back in Attica, the Athenians had returned for the second time to their city, most of which had been systematically destroyed by the Persians in their brief reoccupation that June. Only a few fine houses, where Persian grandees had stayed, were left intact. The city resounded to the noise of frantic rebuilding as Athenians tried to get roofs over their heads before the autumn rains.

Booty from Plataea may have helped some hoplite heroes, but for most citizens it was a very hard time. This did not mean that they could afford to neglect politics, however.

In its unwalled state, Athens was acutely vulnerable to any enemy. Sparta, which famously had no walls but relied on its armies, suggested that a rewalled Athens might become a base for the Persians if they returned. Instead, they suggested that Athens use the Peloponnese as its natural fortress. This argument convinced no one in Athens. But to keep the Spartans away while the Athenians were re-fortifying their city, Themistocles returned to Sparta, where he convinced the Spartans that the Athenians were only rebuilding their homes, not their walls, inviting them to send envoys to see for themselves. The envoys were promptly seized as hostages until the walls were finished.

The crash rebuilding of Athens' walls (only around the inland city itself at this stage) produced walls 8m/25ft high and 2.5m/8ft thick, enough to deter any Greek army at the time. The Spartans, grudgingly accepting this fait accompli, agreed to continue the war against Persia in 478BC.

DISGRACE OF PAUSANIAS

The League's forces were still nominally commanded by Pausanias, the Spartan victor at Plataea. His fleet of 20 triremes joined a much larger Athenian and Ionian force, and they sailed to Cyprus, conquering part of it. They then moved north to Byzantium on the Bosphorus and ejected the Persian garrison from that strategically important city. Meanwhile King Leotychidas of Sparta and Themistocles led a joint land campaign to reconquer northern Greece. Spartan proposals to punish 'medizing' states were blocked by Themistocles, however, who realized that this could boost Sparta's own power.

During 478BC it became apparent that Pausanias, like many Spartans away from domestic austerity, was highly corruptible. At Byzantium he began behaving in ways that were not only autocratic, offending the allies, but also non-Greek. He adopted Persian clothes (wearing purple trousers) and other luxuries and began corresponding secretly with Persian satraps. The Spartan *ephors* finally recalled him, but it was too late for Sparta's prestige. Pausanias' subsequent career ended with his deposition and death by starvation, again revealing Sparta's systemic short-comings. Meanwhile, the Ionian Greeks had turned to Athens for leadership in the continuing war against Persia.

Above: The Hellespontine region (Dardanelles) became a crucial campaigning area after the Persian Wars. Wheat supplies for Athens from the Black Sea had to pass through its straits.

Right: The victorious commander at Plataea, Pausanias, later fell out with other Greeks and his own government. Recalled to Sparta and accused of treason, he was starved to death in a temple where he had sought sanctuary.

THE CONFEDERACY OF DELOS
478–460BC

In the winter of 478–477BC the Confederacy of Delos was established under Athenian leadership. Its aim was to continue the war against Persia. Despite the great victories of the previous two years, there was reason to fear a resurgence of Persian power. The Ionians, repelled by Pausanias' arrogant behaviour, had realized Sparta's inadequacy as a leader in overseas warfare, hence the setting up of the Confederacy. Sparta faced serious problems with Argos and the *helots* (Sparta's slave class) that preoccupied it over the next 20 years.

The Confederacy's headquarters was the small island of Delos in the Cyclades, sacred to Apollo. In its Council, every member from the smallest to the largest (Athens) had one vote. All swore to have "the same friends and enemies", a standard Greek oath, and to continue the alliance "until iron should float" (i.e. forever). This clause later created problems because it offered members no way out.

PAYMENT OF PHOROS
Every city – which from the start included most Ionian and Aeolian cities in Asia Minor, the adjacent islands, most

Above: This serpentine column (now in Istanbul) was set up at Delphi to celebrate Greek victories. Initially it had Pausanias' name on it but this was soon removed.

Below: The new anti-Persian confederacy, formed in 477BC and led by Athens, chose the small Cycladic island of Delos, sacred to the god Apollo, for its headquarters and treasury. The alliance was known as the League or Confederacy of Delos.

Above: The Athenian Aristides, nicknamed 'the Just' for his honesty, became the Delian League's first treasurer, impartially assessing the contributions due from each state.

of the Cyclades and all the Euboean cities except Carystus – made contributions in kind (ships) or in cash. Aristides, renowned for his honesty, became the first treasurer and assessed every *phoros* (contribution). The total revenue from 200 cities came to 460 talents, enough to maintain 100 Confederate galleys. Athens' own fleet had 200 triremes. Revenue was counted by ten Athenian officials called *hellenotamiae* (treasurers of the Greeks). Smaller members found it easier to pay in cash than to equip a trireme. Gradually, more and more members, and especially any who rebelled, moved from being independent contributors of ships to mere *phoros*-payers – a demotion that often caused resentment.

THE LEAGUE
Athens generally favoured democracy in League members, but seldom imposed it without invitation by an internal faction.

Democracy alienated some states' richer citizens, who faced higher taxes under such regimes. Athens later began interfering in tributary members' legal affairs, transferring disputes between members to Athenian law courts. This had advantages – distant Athenian juries were often impartial – but further infringed cities' cherished independence.

THE RISE AND FALL OF CIMON

The Confederacy's early years were glorious. Cimon, son of Miltiades, the victor of Marathon, was Aristides' protégé. As an Athenian *strategos* and leader of the Confederate fleet, he ousted Pausanias from Byzantium, which was enrolled in the Confederacy. In 476BC he attacked the Persian fort of Eion on the River Strymon. Its commander, Boges, held out for a long time, finally immolating himself, his wives and children on a pyre rather than surrender. Cimon failed to take Persian-held Doriscus east along the coast, but in 474BC captured the island of Scyros, a pirate stronghold. The bones of Theseus, the legendary Athenian king, were found there and brought back in triumph. Athens settled *cleruchs* (colonists) on Scyros, the first of many such colonies. Carystus to the south was compelled to join the alliance, and Naxos, when it tried to secede in 469BC, was forcibly prevented – justifiably perhaps, as the war against Persia was continuing.

A convivial, conservative nobleman, Cimon dominated Athenian politics alongside Aristides after Themistocles was ostracized in 471BC. (The great radical had made many enemies, and Athenian politics were volatile.) In 467BC Cimon sailed east and destroyed a new Persian armada of 200 galleys and the accompanying army on the River Eurymedon in southern Asia Minor, ending Persia's hopes of revenge. The cities of Pamphylia and Lycia were then enrolled in the Confederacy. Spoils from the allied victory were used partly to rebuild the Athenian's Acropolis walls – a contentious use. Possibly this provoked

Thasos, a rich island controlling gold mines in Thrace, to revolt in 465BC. It took two years' hard fighting before Cimon could suppress it. Meanwhile, Athenian squadrons, fully professional after years of campaigning, sailed across the eastern Mediterranean unchallenged.

EARTHQUAKE IN SPARTA

When an earthquake in Lacademonia in 464BC triggered a *helot* revolt that the Spartans could not repress, Cimon argued that Athens should help Sparta, still her ally. He led 4,000 Athenian hoplites, noted for their siege skills, to help take Mt Ithome, the *helots'* walled refuge. But the Spartans soon grew alarmed at having democrats inside their country, while Athenians were dismayed to discover the true nature of *helot* serfdom. Humiliatingly, Sparta told the Athenians to leave, but retained its other allies.

This rebuff led to Cimon's ostracism on his return in 461BC, for Ephialtes, a new radical, had emerged to dominate Athenian politics. Soon after, a war broke out that came to divide much of Greece into two hostile camps: Athenian and Spartan. But Athenian power was still expanding. When a fleet campaigning in Cyprus was asked to assist an Egyptian revolt against Persia, it sailed south.

Above: Cimon, son of Miltiades and ally of Aristides, emerged as the chief Athenian strategos after 478BC. He led the League of Delos in a triumphant series of campaigns, driving the Persians from the Aegean. At home Cimon kept open house, entertaining lavishly like the old-style aristocrat he was.

Below: The Portara Gateway, Naxos. In 469BC Naxos tried to quit the League. This attempt was suppressed by Athens, which argued that the war against Persia required all members to keep fighting.

DEMOCRACY'S COMPLETION
462-458 BC

Above: An ostrakon, *a small potsherd used in the yearly poll to decide who should be ostracized (sent into temporary exile), one of the 'safety valves' of democracy devised by Cleisthenes. Many popular leaders, including Themistocles, were ostracized.*

Below: Naval power in the ancient Mediterranean depended on galleys crewed mainly by citizens. Athens' trireme fleets, which ruled the Aegean for much of the 5th century BC, gave seasonal employment to c.30,000 citizen-rowers, forging a link between democracy at home and an aggressive anti-Persian policy abroad that soon became imperialist.

Little is known about Ephialtes, the radical democrat who in 462BC clipped the powers of the Areopagus, the ancient court, and so helped to finalize democracy. His person or policies evidently roused violent passions, however, for he was assassinated soon afterwards – something rare even in Athens' often turbulent democracy.

But Ephialtes' legacy lived on in the career of Pericles, the Alcmaeonid aristocrat who became the greatest democratic statesman in ancient history. Pericles was to guide Athens through nearly 30 years of unparalleled brilliance.

CURBING THE AREOPAGUS

The Council of the Areopagus (named after the Hill of Ares, or Mars, where it sat) retained some powers as well as immense prestige in 462BC. Composed of ex-*archons* after their year in office (all chosen by lot since 487BC), it heard charges against elected officials after their year in power. It also probably supervised the whole body of the law, with wide if undefined powers as the main court of appeal. All this made it a force to be reckoned with, and, with its members still recruited from only the two upper classes, it tended to be conservative.

Ephialtes had paved the way for the reduction of its old powers by accusing several Areopagites of corruption. With Cimon out of sight in Sparta and then ostracized, Ephialtes was able to persuade the Assembly to transfer almost all the Areopagus' powers to itself, either in the form of the Council of Five Hundred or, when constituted as a *heliaea*, as a jury court. (The council and juries were chosen by lot so that they accurately represented the *demos*, the people.) All that was left to the Areopagus was its jurisdiction in murder and arson cases and care of the sacred olive trees. *Archons*, however, still gave a preliminary hearing to lawsuits.

DRAMA AS PROPAGANDA

Powerful propaganda in defence of this democratizing reform came in the form of Aeschylus' last, perhaps greatest, dramatic trilogy, the *Oresteia*, first produced c.458BC. The final play in the trilogy, *Eumenides* (The Kindly Ones), focuses on the plight of Orestes. Guilty of the hideous crime of matricide, Orestes flees from Delphi to Athens pursued by the Furies. On the hill of the Areopagus, Athena, patron goddess of the city, appears, rescues him and founds the Areopagus as a court specifically to deal with such cases. The Furies are then tamed and become the Kindly Ones.

Since Aeschylus, the first of the three great Athenian dramatists, came from the hoplite class (his proudest boast on his tombstone was that he had fought at the Battle of Marathon), his views probably voiced those of many ordinary Athenians.

Ephialtes and Pericles were therefore not considered to be dangerous extremists, but were merely completing the constitutional reforms begun by Cleisthenes 50 years earlier.

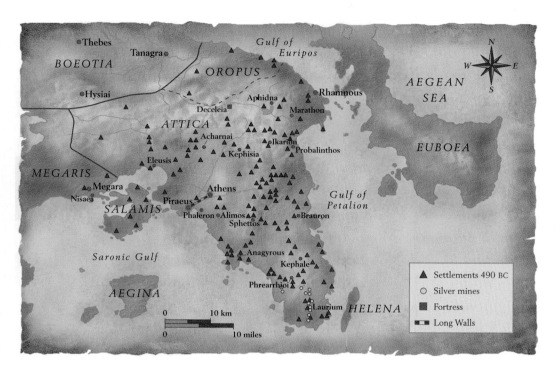

Left: Attica in c.450BC showing the demes (the basic unit of Athenian political and social life after Cleisthenes' democratic reforms of 508BC, on membership of which citizenship depended), the Long Walls and the silver mines at Laurium. Even at its greatest extent, Attica was always hemmed in by potential enemies.

SPREADING POWER

Around the same time, Pericles introduced pay for jurors, probably at a rate of one obol a day, later raised to two. As this was less than the average daily wage, it was not an inducement to idleness (as Aristophanes, the comic playwright, suggested in his play *The Wasps* of 426BC), but it did mean that poverty would not prevent poorer citizens from acting as jurors. In 458BC the *archon*ship also became a paid office to which the *zeugitae* (the middle or hoplite class) now became eligible, so robbing this ancient office, descended from the royal council, of its last aristocratic distinction. There were by this time ten *archons* (literally rulers) of whom three went back to Athens' legendary past: the *basileos*, or king *archon*, with a priestly role; the *polemarch*, originally the military commander; and the eponymous *archon*, who gave his name to the year of his election. Athens dated events by referring to the 'year so-and-so was *archon*'. Later, dating from the first Olympiad (776BC) was adopted.

THE LOTTERY IN ATHENS

Athenians made extensive use of sortition (lotteries) to choose men for many important public posts. In Athens *archons* were chosen by lot after 487BC, as were jurors and other officials. Such a way of choosing officials seems odd today, but there were sound reasons behind it: it reduced the chances of undue influence being brought to bear on anyone; it spread the benefits and the burdens of active citizenship widely; and it was regarded as incorruptible. Elaborate mechanisms for rattling the tokens with the citizens' names on them have been recovered.

Below: The approach to the Acropolis, with the ruins of the temple of Athena Nike (Athena the Victor) standing out to remind citizens of the glories of their city, as it approached its zenith.

THE FIRST PELOPONNESIAN WAR 460–446BC

Above: An Athenian citizen-soldier bidding farewell to his family, a typical scene from the First Peloponnesian War.

Cimon's humiliation broke Athens' last ties with Sparta, though in truth they had long been fraying. While Sparta's growing jealousy of Athens was held in check by *helot* revolts, Athenian power had yet to acknowledge its limits. For a short but intoxicating time, it seemed that Athens would replace Sparta as *hegemon* (leader) of mainland Greece as well as of the Delos Confederacy, while gaining a major role in Egypt. Although such hopes were shattered, Athens emerged undefeated from this First Peloponnesian War, though strained by her experiences.

In 459BC Athens allied with Argos, Sparta's traditional enemy, and settled some Messenians (rebel *helots* whom the Spartans had allowed to leave Mt Ithome) at Naupactus on the Gulf of Corinth. Both were hostile acts. War finally broke out in 459BC when Megara, Athens' small neighbour, quarrelled with Corinth and left the Spartan Alliance, allying instead with Athens. An Athenian expedition helped Megara to build long walls down to its port at Nisaea, so cutting the Isthmus road. Aegina, Athens' old naval rival, was invaded

Left: A relief of Athena mourning by a grave stone. Nobly restrained in her grief, the goddess epitomizes the heroism of Athens at the time, when many citizens died fighting for their city as far away as Egypt.

> ### DIFFERING ALLIANCES: SPARTA VERSUS ATHENS
>
> The Confederacy of Delos, which by 450BC had become an Athenian empire, had started with a formal council. Always dominated by Athens as the strongest member, this disappeared by *c.*450BC. What we term the Peloponnesian League, but which was at the time called 'Sparta and her allies', seems to have had no official organization. Sparta proudly used to point out that – unlike the Athenian Empire, where finally only the two large islands of Lesbos and Chios kept their own fleets – all Sparta's allies maintained their fleets and/or armies, central to their independence. But it would have been awkward for Sparta to levy financial contributions, for most Peloponnesian states supplied armies, not fleets. Sparta could in practice be just as bullyingly exploitative toward her allies as Athens was to hers.

in 458BC and, after a year-long siege, capitulated, being forced into the Confederacy. A diversionary attack by Corinth on Megara was meanwhile repelled by a scratch Athenian force of old men and youngsters.

At around the same time Athens built her own double Long Walls. These linked the city to the booming port of Piraeus, making her almost impregnable to direct land attack, something that Themistocles had long ago wanted. In late 457BC a land battle at Oenophyta saw Boeotia come under Athenian control also – an unusual situation that continued for ten years. Athens then won over Phocis and Locris, small states to the west of Boeotia, parts of Thessaly and the city of Troezen in the Peloponnese.

She seemed set to become the hegemon, the dominant Greek power, on land as well as at sea.

DISASTER IN EGYPT

What offered Athens even greater prospects of power in the 450s BC was Egypt. Immensely rich, Egypt was never happy under Persian rule. Its Persian satrap was killed in an uprising in 459BC led by Inarus, a Libyan who appealed to the Confederate fleet then in Cyprus. The Athenians dispatched a fleet of 200 ships to expel the Persians from Egypt. In return, shiploads of wheat went north to Athens. But in 456BC a Persian army drove the Athenians from Memphis (Cairo), blockading them on an island in the Nile Delta for 18 months. The whole expedition was lost, few of its 40,000 men escaping to distant Cyrene.

CIMON'S RETURN TO VICTORY

Alarmed at this disaster, and fearing a Persian fleet might enter the Aegean, the Athenians transferred the Confederate Treasury to Athens. (Once there, even after the panic ended, it was run conveniently in Athens' interest, one sixtieth of the total revenue being deducted annually as administrative costs.) Cimon, back from his ten-year ostracism, helped to arrange a truce with Sparta and was elected *strategos* to lead another fleet east. This, again 200 ships strong, sailed to Cyprus in 450BC, with 60 ships going to help another revolt in Egypt. They returned for a last victory at Cypriot Salamis, won by Cimon on his deathbed. In 449BC the Peace of Callias was signed between Athens and Persia. By it Athens gave up southern Asia Minor and Cyprus but the Great King agreed to keep Persian troops 80km/50 miles away from the west and north-west coasts, acknowledged as being in the Athenian sphere.

THE 30 YEARS' PEACE

Most of Athens' gains in central Greece soon unravelled: defeats in Boeotia led to its loss, and Phocis and Locris broke away

about then, as did Megara and Euboea. (Oligarchs in these states were generally anti-Athenian).

Only Euboea was finally reconquered after hard campaigning by Pericles. Athens had to abandon all its conquests except Aegina in the 30 Years' Peace of 446BC. This was signed between the Athenian Empire, as it had now become, and the Peloponnesian League.

Above: The Lions at Delos, where the Confederate Treasury was first kept.

Below: Control of the grain routes from the Black Sea remained vital to Athens' survival. Among Greek colonies in the area was Istrus near the Danube Delta.

TOTAL DEMOCRACY
ATHENIAN DEMOCRACY IN ACTION

Below: Athena, maiden goddess of wisdom and the crafts, was very aptly the special deity of Athens, a city Aristotle later called "the city hall of wisdom". Hailed as promachos, *defender or champion, she was often shown with helmet and spear. Her eponymous city repeatedly fought for its existence and glory.*

Democracy (*democratia*) means the rule of the *demos* (the people) – literally so in Athens and other Greek cities that followed her pattern of total democracy. The twin aims of Athenian democracy were to give power to the whole populace and to avoid any individual or group gaining undue power by holding office repeatedly. In practice, this meant elevating amateurism to unprecedented

heights – with results that were far less disastrous than might have been expected. Socrates the philosopher was only one of many critics of such amateurism, however. The great exceptions to this avoidance of experts were the ten annually elected *strategoi* (generals) – posts therefore sought by ambitious men, whether or not they had military talent. Pericles was re-elected as a *strategos* repeatedly (14 times after 443BC), but his power still rested ultimately on votes in the Assembly, which could censure all officials. Thucydides, a superb historian but indifferent general, was exiled for losing a crucial battle.

THE ROLE OF THE ASSEMBLY
The Assembly of all eligible male citizens (*ecclesia*) was literally the government, not a chamber of elected representatives. It listened to foreign ambassadors and voted for war or peace. Any citizen could speak, voicing his opinions before the massed citizenry. (This put an obvious premium on public speaking, and richer citizens from the mid-5th century BC began paying to acquire the rhetorical skills needed to sway the crowds.) Decrees passed by majority vote at each meeting of the Assembly were prominently displayed on whitened boards in the Agora in central Athens so "that any who wished could read them". (Most male Athenians could read a bit, though fewer could write well.)

The Assembly met in the open, originally in the Agora, the commercial and social centre. After 500BC it moved to the Hill of the Pnyx, west of the Acropolis. Speakers stood on a plinth to address the Assembly below on a platform built *c.*400BC, whose remains can be seen today. The Assembly met every nine days on average, although heralds could summon emergency meetings often initiated by

Right: As Athenian democracy reached its zenith, it celebrated its goddess and itself by building the Parthenon, most sublime of Greek temples. In this painting by the Victorian artist Sir Lawrence Alma-Tadema, Pericles is shown visiting the work in progress, talking to the sculptor Pheidias at work on the great frieze.

a *strategos*. To convene a quorum of 6,000 citizens for it, Scythian policemen would drag a cable covered in red dye through the Agora from the north, thus herding citizens into the Assembly. Any citizen who was found outside the Assembly that day with red dye on his clothes faced possible punishment.

THE DISENFRANCHISED

This quorum number of 6,000 was, however, probably only one tenth of the total citizenry at Athens' zenith. Many citizens lived in distant parts of Attica, too far from the city to attend Assembly frequently, while *cleruchs* (settlers) on the islands would seldom have voted. No provision was made to represent these absent citizens in Athens. (Our best information about Athens' constitution comes from Aristotle, the learned, perceptive, sometimes critical 4th-century BC philosopher.)

Metics (registered foreign residents settled in Athens) had no vote, nor could they own property. *Metics* rarely won citizenship, even for outstanding services to the state. Women, slaves and children never had the vote either. So Athenian democracy had its definite limits, especially after the Citizenship Law of 451 BC, which stipulated that both of a citizen's parents had to be Athenian. (This would have excluded Themistocles from citizenship.) The law, proposed by Pericles, met a public desire to limit the benefits of Athenian citizenship and also encouraged *cleruchs* resident overseas to marry Athenian women left at home.

THE COUNCIL AND HELIAEA

Although the Assembly was the sovereign government, the *Boule* (the Council, originally composed of 400 men, though increased to 500 after Cleisthenes' reforms in 507 BC) discussed beforehand what matters would (usually) be debated. The Council was in theory a microcosm of the Assembly. Its members were chosen by lot from all citizens aged 30 or more; none could serve in it more than twice and never in consecutive years, so keeping it amateur. The Council was therefore only a filter for the Assembly, although in the 4th century BC it took a more active role in guiding it. This *probouletic* business was time-consuming, and from 460 BC councillors received modest pay. Most citizens served as councillors at least once. No one, as Pericles said, was excluded from politics because of poverty.

Many would have served more often in a *heliaea* (jury court). These were large courts (at least 201, sometimes 2,001 men), again chosen by lot to avoid corruption or intimidation. As professional lawyers or judges did not exist, plaintiffs and defendants made their cases in person. The jurors, after deciding the verdict by majority voting, decided the penalty too, although the defendant would suggest his own. Almost all Athenian citizens played a civic or political role at some stage, just as all fought in the army or fleet. This was total democracy in action.

Below: After 500 BC the Assembly met at the Hill of the Pnyx, on which stood a plinth. From it speakers addressed the assembled sovereign people.

ATHENS THE EDUCATOR
THE IDEAL CITY

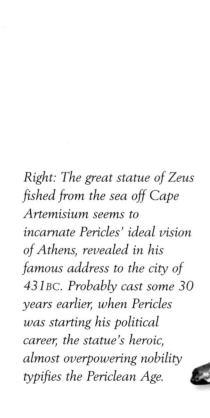

Above: The Parthenon in Athens, erected in the 5th century BC, became the most famous temple in the world.

"Our city is open to the world, we do not at fixed times deport people to prevent them discovering our military secrets. This is because we rely not on hidden weapons but on our courage and loyalty.... We do not let our love of beauty make us extravagant, nor our love of wisdom soften us. We see wealth as something to be used properly, not to boast about. No one needs to be ashamed of being poor: shame lies in doing nothing about it. Everyone is interested not only in their own affairs but in public affairs too, and is well informed about politics. We think that the man who minds only his own business has no business in the city at all. ... Taking everything into account, I declare our city is the educator of Greece."

So spoke Pericles in his funeral oration for Athenian soldiers at the start of the Peloponnesian War in 431BC. He was expressing an ideal of his city, of course (Greeks were given to idealizations), but this vision had found concrete form in the art, drama and architecture of the previous 30 years. This embodiment continued for almost 30 years after his death in 429BC. As Athens flowered, she became the educator of Greece, then later of Rome, and so of the whole Western world. The temples especially, with their statues and other artworks, elevated Athens – celebrating her gods, heroes and herself – to an almost godlike level.

Right: The great statue of Zeus fished from the sea off Cape Artemisium seems to incarnate Pericles' ideal vision of Athens, revealed in his famous address to the city of 431BC. Probably cast some 30 years earlier, when Pericles was starting his political career, the statue's heroic, almost overpowering nobility typifies the Periclean Age.

THE TEMPLES' DEBATE

By ending the long war against Persia, the Peace of Callias in 449BC triggered a debate in Athens about the purpose of her empire, especially about the contributions still paid by subordinate member states. A Panhellenic congress proposed at about this came to nothing, as Sparta predictably refused to attend.

Athens had sworn in 479BC not to rebuild the Acropolis temples burnt down by the Persians until revenged. Their smoke-blackened ruins still dominated the city skyline. Pericles proposed that, with victory won, some of the money used for the fleet should go to rebuilding the city's temples. Athens had sacrificed these (and the rest of her city) for the Panhellenic cause in 480–479BC. Now it was payback time.

Not every Athenian – let alone every subject of the empire – agreed. Thucydides, son of Melesias (not the great historian but his cousin, also related to Cimon), led the opposition in Athens. Other Greeks would feel insulted, he said, when they saw money scheduled for war being used to "gild and adorn our city like a harlot, with costly statues and 1000-talent temples". But Thucydides lost the argument. Temple-building would give employment in Athens for citizens no longer rowing the fleets. Besides, Athenians felt they deserved their city's restoration and decoration. Thucydides was ostracized.

BUILDING THE PARTHENON

In 447BC work began on what has become the most famous temple in the world: the Parthenon, within which rose the huge *chryselephantine* (gold-and-ivory covered) statue of Athena Parthenos, the virgin warrior goddess renowned for wisdom. The Parthenon, which employed the latest techniques of *entasis* – by which columns curved in to appear regular in size when seen from afar – was mainly designed by Ictinus, and completed in 432BC. The statue of Athena, and the carvings of the frieze depicting the

Pan-Athenaic Procession running around the Parthenon (some of which are now the Elgin Marbles in the British Museum) were the work of Pheidias. Both men were supreme geniuses.

SUPERSTITION TO PHILOSOPHY

Pericles served prominently on the commission overseeing work on the Parthenon. Pheidias was one of his friends. So, more controversially, was Anaxagoras from Clazomenae, a philosopher who taught that the sun was only a vast hot stone – "bigger than the Peloponnese" – and not divine. This struck some people as impious, even tempting fate. Protagoras of Abdera, another philosopher, proclaimed: "Man is the measure of all things!" Pericles, who believed in an exalted equality, shrugged off old superstitions in the bright noon of Athenian democracy, as the city drew the greatest minds of the Greek world to her.

Above: The frieze depicting the grand Pan-Athenaic Procession running around the Parthenon was carved under the direction of Pheidias, one of the greatest sculptors of classical Greece.

Right: Theseus Diadoumenus *is the work of another brilliant but very different sculptor of High Classicism, Polyclitus of Argos, who often worked in Athens. His statue shows the legendary Athenian king as a perfectly proportioned young man. (Polyclitus was obsessed with mathematical proportion.) This is a Roman copy of a Greek original.*

THE RICH PAY FIRST

There was no regular income tax in Athens. Instead, most great festivals, and many of the triremes, were financed by the 1,200 or so richest citizens. These Athenians who chose, or were chosen, to finance a particular event did not simply pay for particular dramas (the *choregeia*) or religious festivals: they had to put them on, recruiting and rehearsing the actors and musicians needed. These demands were called *liturgia* (public burdens). For a *trierarch*, his liturgy meant building, equipping, crewing and commanding a trireme – a great effort. But love of honour and *areté* (excellence) drove wealthy Athenians to compete with each other in such active munificence in the 5th century BC.

CHAPTER IV

WORLD WAR IN MINIATURE

431–404BC

The Peloponnesian War marked a turning point in Greek history. Before it, Athens seemed set on an upward trajectory, which could have led to most of Greece becoming united under its leadership. Afterwards, although Greek civilization continued to develop, any such possibility vanished. The long wars between 431 and 404BC affected almost all the Greek world, half-ruining much of it. We call it the Peloponnesian War, showing our Athenian perspective; for Sparta and its allies, it was the Athenian War. It has been called a world war in miniature, as important as the Persian Wars.

The war divides into two stages. In the first, 431–421BC, the Spartans often tried to attack, although they had only one brilliant general, Brasidas, whose death led to an uneasy peace. This was broken by the Athenian attack on Syracuse in 415BC. Defeat in Sicily imperilled Athens' overseas empire and its democracy at home. Athenian democracy showed itself at its worst in rejecting peace offers until final defeat. Thucydides' superb history covers the war to 411BC. If not impartial, writing with only just controlled passion, he is searchingly intelligent. His words sum up the war: 'The Peloponnesian War not only lasted a long time, but brought with it unprecedented suffering for Hellas. Never before had so many cities been captured and then devastated; never before had so many people been exiled or lost their lives.'

Left: The funerary stele of Chareidemos and Lykeas, two Athenian hoplites among the many killed in the war.

SIEGE, PLAGUE AND REBELLION 431–427BC

Below: At the outset of war in 431BC, Athens was at its political and cultural peak, as masterworks such as this Amazon, copy of an original by Pheidias, shows.

In late May 431BC, "when the wheat was ripe", an unstoppable 30,000-strong Spartan-led army rolled into Attica, burning everything in its path. It was trying to provoke the Athenians, crammed behind their walls, to come out and fight. They did not, and after a month Sparta's Peloponnesian allies, who made up most of the army but lacked *helots* (Sparta's slave class) to work their farms, insisted on returning home.

SIEGE OF PLATAEA

Over the border in Boeotia, Plataea, allied to Athens, was besieged by Thebes. Thebes had jumped the gun in March by trying to seize Plataea in a night attack. The coup failed, the Theban infiltrators were killed and Plataea's civilians evacuated to Athens. Then the Theban army arrived to besiege the tiny city. It took four years before it fell. All the surviving garrison was killed and the city razed to the ground – a vicious start to the war. Meanwhile, Athenian ships raided the Peloponnese around Troezen to little effect. However, the speech that Pericles made at the funeral of the Athenian soldiers first exalted democracy to the sublime levels of the Elgin marbles, at least according to Thucydides who heard it. "Individual Athenians adapt to every different sort of action with versatility and grace. We have raised marvellous monuments to our power. Future ages will wonder at us, and we need no Homer and his poems to praise us.

Our courage has blazed paths across every sea and land. This is the city for which these men nobly fought and died."

THE PLAGUE

In 430BC disaster struck Athens in a way that Pericles had not foreseen: plague, reputedly from Egypt, which kept recurring. It was probably smallpox, judging by Thucydides' graphic description. (He had it himself, noted the symptoms with clinical detachment, and recovered.) It hardly affected the land-locked Peloponnese, but it killed nearly one-third of Athens' population of *c.*175,000 crowded together.

PERICLES' FALL AND RETURN

This was the first, and in some ways worst, disaster of the war, and the people turned on Pericles as a scapegoat. An attack he led had failed to capture Epidaurus, its target. He lost office, was

INEFFECTUAL SIEGE CRAFT

Despite being supreme on land, like the Spartans, or at sea, like the Athenians, the Greeks before 400BC were oddly inept at siege warfare. Compared to contemporary Persians or to monarchs of the 4th century such as Alexander the Great, they often seemed powerless before any well-built, well-defended wall. If surprise attack or treachery (or the two combined) failed, blockading a city until it starved was the normal way to capture it. Greek armies had battering rams and ladders and might try mining under walls or even primitive flame-throwers, but they lacked other siege engines. Only in the 4th century did Sicilian and Macedonian rulers revolutionize siege warfare with powerful catapults and gigantic siege towers.

Right: War required all citizens of military age (between 18 and 60) to serve in the fleet or army. Here Pericles, rather fancifully, is depicted fighting alongside his friend the sculptor Pheidias. In fact, Pheidias left Athens soon after the war's start and Pericles, as leading strategos, *commanded the fleet.*

accused of corruption and fined. Pheidias, his friend the great sculptor, was also fined. Another friend, the philosopher Anaxagoras, had to flee the city and return to his native Lampsacus after questioning the gods' existence, an act of dangerous impiety in troubled times. Even Pericles' mistress Aspasia, who had joined their dinner parties (very few women did), was prosecuted.

But Athenian public opinion swung back and Pericles was reinstated as *strategos*. Meanwhile, campaigns in two important areas, the Gulf of Corinth, and around the Chalcidic peninsula in the north, had mixed results. Demosthenes (the 5th-century BC *strategos*, not the 4th century orator) led not unsuccessful operations in the west, although he lost many men in them.

THE REVOLT OF LESBOS

In 428BC the oligarchical government of Mytilene on Lesbos revolted, taking most of the island with it. Lesbos, which was still a free ally of Athens, had no specific complaints, so its revolt was a huge shock. To pay for its suppression, a novel property tax, the *eisphora*, was introduced. Mytilene appealed to Sparta, which sent one adviser. By May 427BC the Lesbian leaders, under pressure from their starving people, finally had to surrender to the Athenian forces.

On the news of their surrender, a great debate arose in the Assembly about how to treat the rebels. Cleon, now the leading radical, urged that all male citizens on Lesbos should be executed. His proposal was carried, and a galley sailed with the grim news. But another politician, Diodotus, persuaded an extraordinary Assembly meeting to be merciful (on the

pragmatic grounds that the Lesbian *people* had not revolted) and another galley was sent in hot pursuit. It reached Lesbos just in time and only the ringleaders were executed. But most land on Lesbos was allocated to Athenian *cleruchs*. As absentee landlords, they let it out to locals, who had to pay rent for farms that had previously been their own.

Below: While most Peloponnesian states followed the Spartan-led alliance, most islands and ports were part of Athens' empire, making the war look like one between land and sea. But there were exceptions such as Corinth, a great pro-Spartan port.

Athenian Allies
Athens & her Empire
Sparta & allied states
Neutral states

SPARTA'S DEFEAT AND PEACE
425–421BC

Below: This superb Nike (statue of victory) is one of the first semi-nude female statues in classical art. The marble statue was made by Paionius for the Messenians of Naupactus, celebrating the part they played in the Athenian victory over Sparta in 425BC.

Athens had seldom contemplated attacking the Peloponnese on its south-west flanks. It had only one ally, Zacynthus, in the area, yet Achaea and Aetolia, south and north of the Corinthian Gulf, were friendly neutrals and at Naupactus near the Gulf's mouth lived *helots* from Messenia, who were fanatically loyal to Athens. A civil war, waged with appalling savagery, led to the Corcyran democrats regaining control of most of the island. An Athenian squadron sailed to Sicily in 428BC in response to Ionian cities' appeal for protection against their Doric neighbours.

SURRENDER AT PYLOS

The Athenian *strategos* Phormion had defeated larger Peloponnesian squadrons in 429BC in the Corinthian Gulf by dazzling seamanship. (On one occasion Athenian galleys forced the enemy fleet to form a defensive circle with bows pointed outward. Around this, Athenian triremes rowed closer and closer, forcing their enemies inward to foul their oars.) After Phormion's death, in 426BC Demosthenes, another adventurous *strategos*, saved the *helots* of Naupactus from a Spartan attack. Next year, although no longer *strategos*, he accompanied a fleet bound for Sicily. This was blown into the Bay of Pylos on Messenia's west coast by a storm. Demosthenes persuaded the sailors to

Above: The capture of 140 Spartiates (full Spartans) on the Island of Sphacteria in 425BC by Athenian general Demosthenes horrified Sparta and led it to sue for peace – an offer Athens rejected. The war then resumed.

build fortifications on the peninsula of Pylos. Then the main fleet sailed on west, leaving Demosthenes with a small force.

Horrified at the presence of Athenians on Spartan soil, Sparta sent a fleet and troops to eject them. Some 420 Spartiates (Spartan's elite ruling class) with *helot* attendants occupied Sphacteria island to the south. But the wooded Pylos peninsula proved very defensible. Demosthenes' men, although outnumbered, repelled Spartan attacks by land and sea. Brasidas was badly wounded while disembarking.

The Athenian fleet, which had turned back on hearing the news, swept into Pylos Bay to defeat the Spartan ships.

Now the Spartans on Sphacteria, themselves besieged, faced starvation. Among them there happened to be some very important Spartiates.

Sparta, panic-stricken, proposed a truce. To ensure that food was supplied to the marooned Spartiates, it handed over 60 ships and sent envoys to Athens, suggesting peace on the status quo ante as in 431BC. Urged by Cleon, the Assembly rejected this proposal, but kept the 60 ships on a technicality. War resumed, with well-bribed *helots* swimming across to Sphacteria by night with food for the besieged Spartiates. But when Cleon arrived with Athenian reinforcements, including light-armed troops, they stormed Sphacteria at night. Athenian archers and javelin throwers harassed the exhausted Spartans until they surrendered. About 140 Spartiates became prisoners.

This unprecedented Spartan surrender, amazing all of Greece, boosted Athenian self-confidence dangerously. They seized Cythera, an island off Sparta's south coast to which some *helots* had managed to escape. (But Athens never attempted to rouse the resentful *helot* serfs inside Lacedaemonia, which might really have crippled Sparta.) Cleon, aggressively imperialistic, produced a new, heavier tribute list for the empire, often doubling subject cities' *phoros* (taxes). But trouble was growing in the north.

THE LOSS OF AMPHIPOLIS

Amphipolis, founded by Athens in 436BC on the River Strymon by the Macedonian border, was a key city for the empire, controlling a bridge, trade routes and gold mines. In 424BC Brasidas marched north, with no Spartiates but only 700 *helots* armed as hoplites (presumably promised their liberty). He gathered other troops en route to a stunning series of victories. These were won by diplomatic as much as military means, Brasidas having great, if menacing, charm. Some Chalcidic cities were disgruntled with Athenian rule and Brasidas initially had the backing

of the Macedonian king Perdiccas. When Brasidas reached Amphipolis after marching through a winter night, he offered its citizens such easy terms that they surrendered. Thucydides, the *strategos* commanding a squadron at Thasos, hastily sent ships in support, but too late.

Back in Athens, Thucydides was exiled (not ostracized) for the loss. This was perhaps unfair, as he had lacked the forces needed to defend the long north coast against Brasidas, Sparta's best general. Athens, defeated in a hoplite battle by Thebes at Delium in 424BC, had ignored Brasidas' campaign until it was too late. Cleon finally was sent as *strategos* with a decent force – 1,200 Athenian hoplites plus allies – in 422BC to stop Brasidas from winning more cities. In a battle outside Amphipolis, Brasidas and Cleon were both killed, leading to peace in 421BC.

THE PEACE OF NICIAS

Intended to last for 50 years, the Peace of Nicias – named after the conservative Athenian politician – attempted a return to the status quo ante. Athens returned all gains except Nisaea, Megara's port, being promised the return of Amphipolis and other northern cities. (She never got them.) Sparta returned her conquests, but the peace marked a defeat for her. Her allies refused to accept it, accusing Sparta of neglecting the Alliance's interests.

Above: The Temple to Hephaestus, built c.440BC, overlooked the Agora, Athens' social centre.

Below: Trapped on the island of Sphacteria, the Spartans effectively became hostages in their own territory thanks to Athenian tactical brilliance.

THE FALSE PEACE
421–415BC

Above: The debauched features of Alcibiades as imagined by an artist of the Roman period. The flamboyant aristocrat of the Alcmaeonid family led Athens into disastrous adventures.

When agreeing to the Peace of Nicias, Sparta was acutely conscious that the 30 Years' Peace with Argos, her old rival in the Peloponnese, was about to end. Argos had recovered from the devastating defeat in 457BC, but needed help to challenge Sparta, still the region's powerful *hegemon*. As Argos was now a democracy, Athens was the obvious choice. Many younger Athenians were bored with a peace that offered no chances of gain or glory.

ALCIBIADES' RISE TO POWER
The young Alcibiades (born *c*.450BC) now emerged as a prominent figure in Athenian public life. An Alcmaeonid and former ward of Pericles, he had been wounded while fighting bravely at the Battle of Potidaea in 430BC. His life had been saved by Socrates, a fellow hoplite who became a friend. In alliance with the radical Hyperbolus, Alcibiades, handsome, rich and flamboyant, began to dominate the Assembly. Elected *strategos* in 420BC, he persuaded Athens to ally with Argos and other states in the Peloponnese against Sparta. But the Assembly did not choose Alcibiades as *strategos* for the army sent to Argos in 419BC, which proved a mistake. After numerous manoeuvres, King Agis of Sparta defeated the joint Athenian-Argive army at Mantinea in 418BC, which, as Thucydides said, "wiped out the disgrace of Pylos". It also triggered regime change back in Argos. Under a new oligarchy, it allied with Sparta, which recovered its own self-confidence.

In Athens, Alcibiades also switched sides, forming an alliance with the conservative Nicias. Their supporters combined to ostracize Hyperbolus in 418BC, leaving Alcibiades undisputed leader of the radical democrats, who were also the keenest imperialists. This was no paradox: the prospect of employment as rowers in the fleet or of becoming *cleruchs* (colonists) made imperialism especially attractive to the *thetes* (the poorest class). Nicias, never a good general, led an unsuccessful expedition to regain Amphipolis, but Alcibiades was really looking elsewhere.

THE CAPTURE OF MELOS
Melos was a small Cycladic island that had managed to stay out of the Athenian Empire. Neither wealthy nor of much strategic value, it refused to submit to Athens, which accordingly sent a fleet and army to take it in 416BC. Athens must

Left: The Erechtheum, a temple rivalling the Parthenon in ingenuity and elegance if not size, was started in 421BC after the Peace of Nicias. It was only completed in 405BC, the year of Athens' final disastrous defeat.

A FOREWARNING OF DISASTER?

Just before the fleet was due to sail for Sicily, the city was shaken by a great scandal. Many herms (the good-luck statues set outside most houses and temples) were found mutilated one morning. Alcibiades was suspected of being behind this – almost certainly wrongly, considering his prospective command. He was, however, widely seen as a dangerous freethinker, known to frequent scandalous dining-clubs such as the *cacodaemonistae* (evil-spirit worshippers). He demanded, but did not get, an immediate full trial, at which he might have been acquitted. Despite the Athenian public's concern, Alcibiades remained a *strategos* and embarked for Sicily.

have expected an easy victory, but the Melians, though vastly outnumbered, fought back. It took a long siege and Athenian reinforcements before Melos was captured. As was the custom, all Melian men of military age were killed, their women and children enslaved and their land given to 500 Athenian *cleruchs*.

The most interesting aspect of this small campaign was the debate beforehand between the Athenian envoys and Melian magistrates, to which Thucydides devoted nearly a whole chapter. In it, the Athenian envoys propounded a nakedly self-interested imperialism that the historian deplored and few Greeks at the time would have defended so openly.

THE LURE OF SICILY

Sicily has been called the Greek America. It was a land of huge potential wealth and power and a major grain exporter, chiefly to the Peloponnese. But its cities were very Greek in their constant wars. This gave an expansionist Athens opportunities. It had sent small fleets west in the 420s BC to assist Ionian cities against Doric neighbours, and to keep Sicilians too

Right: Nike Unlacing Her Sandal: *this superb statue of victory came originally from the Temple of Athena Nike on the Acropolis. It was begun in* c.428BC *and finished during the brief peace, when Athens indeed seemed victorious.*

preoccupied to help Sparta. But at a congress at Gela in 424BC, Hermocrates, the democratic leader of Syracuse, persuaded the Sicilians not to let outsiders such as Athens meddle in their affairs. Faced with this 'Monroe Doctrine' (excluding old Greece from western Greek affairs), the Athenian fleet returned home.

By the year 415BC, however, much had changed. Egesta, a city in Sicily's extreme west, appealed for help against its neighbour Selinus, an ally of Syracuse. Athenian envoys sent to investigate returned with tales of Egesta's fabulous wealth. These stirred dreams of easy riches in the Assembly and, swayed by Alcibiades, it voted to help Egesta. Nicias warned against so risky a project, but this only led to the force being doubled and he himself was appointed a *strategos*, with Alcibiades and Lamachus. Alcibiades sailed in June 415BC as one of the three *strategoi* commanding the armada. It had 134 triremes and transport ships with 30,000 infantry but almost no cavalry.

Right: The Valley of the Temples in Sicily. The island became a land of huge potential wealth and power and a major exporter of grain, chiefly to the Peloponnese.

DISASTER IN SICILY
415–413 BC

Arriving in the west, the Athenians found a cool reception at Rhegium (Reggio), on the Strait of Messina. They also discovered that Egesta had deceived them about its wealth: it was not rich at all. But, as there could be no ignominious speedy return, a council of war debated the likely options. Nicias suggested arbitrating between Egesta and Selinus, then sailing around the island before returning; Alcibiades wanted a diplomatic initiative to win allies; Lamachus, the one soldier among the *strategoi*, urged an immediate knockout blow at Syracuse, the real enemy. He failed to convince the others, however, and the Athenian fleet cruised down the coast past Syracuse, capturing one Syracusan trireme.

Athenian troops finally landed late in the season in Syracuse's Great Harbour. Here they had a success, their seasoned hoplites defeating the Syracusan army despite the latter's superior cavalry. But Nicias, senior *strategos*, then sailed the army back to Catania for the winter, which was spent trying to find allies rather than preparing for war.

ALCIBIADES' ESCAPE
While the Athenian fleet cruised past Syracuse, a state galley arrived for Alcibiades. He was being recalled to Athens, accused of profaning the Eleusinian Mysteries, the holiest and most revered of all ritual celebrations in Athens. Eluding his captors, he disappeared, to be next heard of in Sparta. His recall was the work of enemies in Athens, where he was soon tried and condemned in absentia.

WALLS AND COUNTER WALLS
In spring 414BC the Athenians returned suddenly, caught the Syracusans off guard and seized part of Epipolae, the plateau to the west. Control of this large plateau now became central to the siege, for through it ran all roads going north. As the Athenian fleet was still superior at sea, cutting these roads would isolate Syracuse. To achieve this, the Athenians began building a double wall with a circular fort at its centre.

Syracuse was led by Hermocrates, a democratic leader comparable to Pericles, but his position remained precariously dependent on success. For the moment it looked as if the Syracusans faced defeat. Although they started to build cross walls to cut off the Athenians in turn, they were slower builders. (How much of the mainland city, as opposed to Ortygia, the citadel, was walled remains uncertain.)

Lamachus was killed during fighting around the walls, leaving the indecisive Nicias as the sole *strategos*. However, Nicias had important contacts inside Syracuse who could, he hoped, deliver the city peacefully to him. In fact, the Syracusan Assembly was about to consider peace negotiations when a Spartan force slipped past the Athenians into the city, commanded by a Spartiate of unusual energy: Gylippus.

Above: Procles Saying Farewell to his Father, a scene typical of Athens in wartime when every citizen did his military service, and many did not return.

Below: Crucial to besieging Syracuse were the heights of Epipolae above the city, where the fortress of Euryalus stood. Failing to hold this point, the Athenians were doomed.

Gylippus breathed new heart into the defence. The strong point at Labdalum was captured, an Athenian trireme taken in the Great Harbour and a new cross wall started on the northern plateau. Remarkably complacent, Nicias ignored this and instead built a fort at Plemmyrium, south of the Great Harbour, to facilitate supplies. But the Athenians were losing the cross-wall race. In a battle on Epipolae Heights, Gylippus worsted the Athenians and completed the third cross wall past the Athenians, cutting them off from land routes. Encouraged, the Syracusans began training their own large fleet, which until then had hidden from the Athenians. As fighting would be in the confined waters of the Great Harbour, the Syracusans strengthened their triremes' prows.

REINFORCEMENTS ARRIVE

Nicias wrote home despairingly in late 414BC, calling for reinforcements or recall. The Assembly, loath to abandon its Sicilian dreams, voted to send a second force of 73 ships and 15,000 men under Demosthenes. Before it arrived, the Syracusan fleet sallied forth and, in a series of engagements, damaged many Athenian ships crammed tightly together, as well as Athenian morale. This was already low because their camp on the beach near the marshes was in an unhealthy malarial spot. But the arrival of Demosthenes in 413BC with his large force alarmed the Syracusans.

RETREAT AND DISASTER

Demosthenes realized that only swift action could save the Athenians. He launched a night attack on the cross walls, which, after initial success, ended in chaotic disaster. As reinforcements could now enter Syracuse freely, Demosthenes urged immediate withdrawal by sea. Nicias hesitated until two naval defeats by the Syracusans – who closed off the Great Harbour – forced him to agree to a retreat, though by land. But an eclipse of the moon caused the superstitious Nicias to delay this plan for a month.

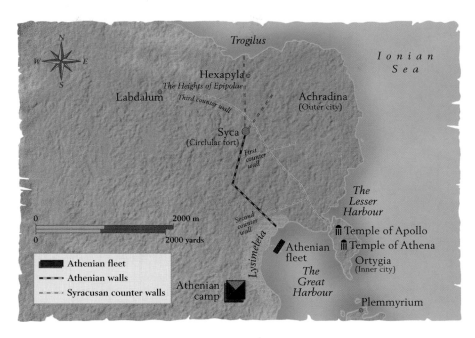

When the Athenians at last began their retreat, with only c.20,000 men left, the Syracusans harassed them continuously. Athenian discipline finally broke as they scrambled down to a river desperate for water, and their army surrendered.

Nicias and Demosthenes were killed, most of the rest becoming slaves in the mines. There many died in appalling conditions, although some reputedly won freedom by reciting lines from Euripides, the Athenian playwright already known in Sicily. Athens' western venture had ended in disaster with the loss of 40,000 men and 200 ships.

Above: Syracuse, on its island citadel, was hard to besiege. The Athenians tried to cut the city off by building a wall, but Syracusans under the dynamic Spartan Gyllipus built a cross wall that cut them off instead.

Below: Oarsmen in a Greek trireme. Control of the seas was always vital to Athenian power. When all the Athenians' ships were destroyed at Syracuse, they were effectively doomed.

AFTER SYRACUSE
REACTION AND REVIVAL, 413–408 BC

Above: From Sardis, Persia's regional capital, Tissaphernes the Persian satrap watched the Greek world, aiming to exploit Greek divisions to regain long-lost territories.

Below: The Council of 400 that replaced democracy did little except build a fort at Piraeus, whose ruins are depicted here by J.R. Herbert, a 19th-century artist. The Council soon gave way to a revived democracy.

Events in Syracuse were to have huge repercussions back in Greece. In Sparta, Alcibiades, who had evaded his Athenian captors, impressed his dour hosts, eating Sparta's revolting black broth with gusto and saying that all Athenian aristocrats considered democracy an 'acknowledged folly'. He gave the Spartans dangerously good advice: they should send an adviser to Syracuse as requested. And they should reinvade Attica, not returning home after a month's ravaging, but instead occupying the fort of Deceleia all year round.

Deceleia was 16km/10 miles north of Athens, well placed to menace the city. Its permanent Spartan garrison prevented Athenian farmers from returning to cultivate their land, as in the war's first part, and it cut the overland road to Euboea. (Some Athenian farmers had moved livestock to that island.) Worse, Deceleia attracted *c.*20,000 runaway slaves over the next decade, often skilled workers vital to the Athenian economy, as a result of which the Laurium silver mines, dependent on slaves, were abandoned.

OLIGARCHIC IDEAS
Aristocratic opposition to democracy went underground during Pericles' ascendancy. Aristocrats benefited from the empire as victorious generals or from overseas properties. But long wars led to higher taxes, such as the *eisphora* (property tax), which hit the richest. Disgusted by the rise of common (if wealthy) men such as Cleon, some aristocrats longed for the 'good old days' before democracy. One anonymous aristocrat, called The Old Oligarch although he was probably young, wrote a pamphlet, *Athenian Constitution*, *c.*424BC. Its importance lies less in sneers against democracy ("the common people dress as badly as slaves") than in showing how strong oligarchical sentiment always remained.

In Athens there was a revulsion against all regarded as responsible for the disaster, be they radical democrats or fortune-tellers – in fact almost anyone

except the ordinary Athenians who had really voted for the expedition, as Thucydides noted dryly. The emergency reserve of 1,000 talents and 100 triremes was broached, and a Board of Ten older men, including the octogenarian playwright Sophocles, supplemented the long-established Council of 500.

GROWING REVOLTS

The Athenian defeat at Syracuse roused the hopes of many people who were discontented with Athenian power. In Lesbos, oligarchs planning to revolt appealed to Sparta and this time got a response: King Agis, realizing Lesbos's proximity to the vital grain trade route, sent a fleet of 100 ships to the eastern Aegean in 412BC. Its arrival triggered revolts in Chios and Ionian cities. In addition, Sparta – again on Alcibiades' advice – had approached Tissaphernes, satrap of Sardis. Persia had adhered to the Peace of Callias, keeping away from the Aegean coast, but Athens had rashly annoyed the Great King by supporting a rebel, and Persia still wanted its former territories back. By the Treaty of Miletus in 412BC, Sparta apparently agreed to Persian claims over all Greek states ever under its rule, in return for money.

Alcibiades arrived that winter in Sardis. His seduction of King Agis' wife meant he was no longer welcome in Sparta, but he charmed Tissaphernes. Alcibiades suggested that regime change in Athens might work to Persia's advantage and he was the man to effect it. He made contacts with the Athenian fleet at Samos. This was manned chiefly by *thetes*, the poorest Athenians, but even they, disillusioned by defeat, now listened briefly to talk of oligarchy, which might win Athens vital Persian gold.

Many middle-of-the-road Athenians, led by Theramenes, felt a change in the constitution was needed, although Athens had responded vigorously to recent revolts, recruiting and dispatching a new fleet. Aristophanes' comic play *Lysistrate*, produced in spring 411BC, depicting Athens' women refusing sex to their husbands unless they made peace, voiced general

war-weariness. After some democratic radicals were murdered amid growing terror, it was proposed that the franchise be restricted to the 5,000 richest citizens. Meanwhile, a Council of 400 would rule, the Assembly being abolished. "It was no small thing to destroy the Athenian people's freedom after 100 years of democracy," commented Thucydides, but the 400's rule, from June to September 411BC, revealed their shortcomings. They built a fort at Piraeus and made unsuccessful peace overtures to Sparta. Meanwhile, Alcibiades, crossing to Samos, won over the Athenian fleet. This declared itself the true Assembly and went on the offensive, led by Thrasyllus and Thrasybulus.

DEMOCRACY RESTORED

Two naval victories led to the restoration of democracy in Athens. The first at Cynossema in late 411BC restored Athenian morale; the more decisive one at Cyzicus (in the sea of Marmara) in the spring of 410BC annihilated the Peloponnesian fleet, despite Persian support. Sparta now offered peace on the basis of the status quo – an offer rejected by the Assembly, now again sovereign in Athens, as the 400 had been overthrown.

Above: A hoplite in an elaborate helmet. All major land battles were decided by these heavy-armed infantry.

Below: The dangerous charm and charisma of Alcibiades, who long bedazzled Athens, comes over well in this Roman copy of a Greek original.

THE FALL OF THE ATHENIAN EMPIRE 408–404 BC

Above: The Piraeus was Athens' great port and its lifeline, for the city was crucially dependent on wheat, which was imported from the Black Sea through the Hellespont.

Alcibiades had overstated his influence with Tissaphernes to the Athenians. That devious Persian satrap, wanting to keep Sparta and Athens involved in mutually exhausting wars, dangled the prospects of Persian alliance – and gold – before both.

ALCIBIADES' RETURN TO ATHENS

Despite gaining no Persian alliance, Alcibiades retained immense appeal for the Athenians. He seemed to be the one man who might still win them the war. Gaining command of the main Athenian fleet, now in the north, he retook Chrysopolis and Chalcedon on the Bosphorus. Then in 408BC he recaptured Byzantium, usually thought impregnable on its peninsula. This ensured safe passage for ships carrying vital wheat from the Black Sea through the Bosphorus to Athens. It was time for his triumphant return to Athens.

Alcibiades reached Athens in June 407BC. His popularity surged yet higher when he gave a ceremonial military escort to the religious procession down the Sacred Way to Eleusis. (For years the Athenians had been going by ship to avoid the Spartans.) Alcibiades was now elected *strategos autocrator* (supreme commander), a role denied even Pericles. Returning to take control of the fleet, however, he made a disastrous mistake. Going off possibly to raise revenue – Athens was desperately short of cash – he left the rest of the fleet under the command of Antiochus, an experienced sailor but a drunk. Antiochus provoked and lost an unnecessary battle to the Spartans at Notion in spring 406BC. With his reputation now shattered, Alcibiades thought it wiser to retire to his castle on the Hellespont.

THE COSTLY VICTORY

The Spartan fleet was now commanded by a new *navarch* (admiral), Lysander, an unusually formidable Spartan. Lysander befriended the youthful Prince Cyrus, known as Cyrus the Younger, who had far-ranging powers. Cyrus soon committed Persia to Sparta, which in turn agreed to Persian demands. With Persian gold, Lysander could hire rowers at better rates than Athens, soon building up a large professional fleet.

But Athens was not defeated yet. Lysander was replaced as *navarch* by the less competent Callicratidas. At Arginusae, south of Lesbos, in late 406BC, the Athenians defeated the Spartan fleet again in a hard-fought battle. But in a storm at the battle's end, many Athenian sailors whose triremes had been sunk

Left: In 405–404BC, during the last winter of the war, the Spartans blockaded a starving Athens until finally the city surrendered.

were left to drown. When the news reached Athens, the Assembly, dominated by Cleophon, another demagogue, became hysterical. (Many had lost friends or relatives in this disaster.) The Assembly tried six *strategoi* for incompetence for not rescuing the drowning men. Among those found guilty and executed were Thrasyllus, Athens' best general at the time, and Pericles the Younger. Such collective trials were almost certainly illegal, but only Socrates the philosopher was brave enough to protest, nearly being lynched in the process.

Athens had now exiled or killed its last good leaders. Cleophon also persuaded the Assembly to reject further Spartan peace offers. Reportedly, he was drunk at the time.

ENDGAME AT GOAT'S RIVERS

Lysander, resuming command of the Spartan fleet in 405BC, took a 200-strong Peloponnesian fleet up to the Hellespont and captured Lampsacus on the south of the Straits, where he stationed his fleet in August. The Athenians, gathering all their ships, pulled up their fleet opposite him on the exposed beach of Aegospotami, Goat's Rivers. It was not a good spot, as supplies had to be brought every day from Sestos, 4.5km/3 miles away. Every day the Athenians rowed out to try to force a battle, but the Spartans refused. Alcibiades rode down from his castle to warn the Athenians to move, but they ignored him.

After four days, the Athenians had returned to cook lunch on the beach when Lysander's fleet sailed over. He caught the Athenians defenceless, taking their ships almost without a fight. About 4,000 Athenian sailors were summarily killed. So complete was the Spartan victory (only 20 ships under Conon escaped) that treachery was suspected. It meant the final end of Athenian seapower, and doomed the city.

The news reached Athens at nightfall, a night 'on which no man slept'. Lysander took his time, sweeping around the

Right: Athena, patron goddess of Athens, thanking Hera, patron goddess of Samos. The carving of 402BC celebrates the fact that Samos was one of the few cities that remained loyal to Athens until the war's bitter end.

Aegean and sending in all Athenian *cleruchs* to swell the numbers of starving citizens. Cleophon again vetoed the first peace proposals. Then the Assembly turned on him and had him executed for evading military service.

As the Spartan blockade tightened, a conference was called among the victors to decide on Athens' fate. Thebes and Corinth wanted the city destroyed, but the Spartans, thinking back to the Persian Wars, would not agree. Instead, Athens had to pull down the Long Walls to Piraeus, give up all overseas possessions, accept the return of all exiles, surrender all but 12 ships and accept a Spartan garrison.

In April 404BC Athens capitulated and Lysander entered the city in triumph. The long war was over.

Below: The theatre of Dionysus, where Athens, despite the disasters – political, social, economic – of a war being lost, continued to produce some of the world's greatest tragedies.

CHAPTER V

THE GREEKS:
THE FIRST INDIVIDUALS
c.650BC–AD147

The Greeks were among the first people about whose lives, loves and luck we can still read with interest and sympathy. This is partly due to the histories and biographies that survive (many have not). But it is also because the Greek *polis* gave some men, if few women, far more scope to be individuals than earlier absolutist monarchies had. Only in Sparta, that dour militaristic state, were there few individuals. Among the Macedonian monarchs, ruling huge empires after Alexander's conquest of Asia, glamorous personalities emerged, although none competes with Alexander himself.

The Greeks tended to hero-worship great generals, athletes, artists and poets. This tendency led, from the 4th century BC, to proclaiming victorious generals or monarchs as gods. This seductive flattery continued into the Roman Empire. Average Athenians must have looked very different from the godlike beings, with perfectly proportioned bodies and features, depicted in the friezes on the Acropolis, but Greeks revered those more blessed than themselves. A Greek *polis* was composed of gods and semi-divine heroes as well as living men.

Counterbalancing such hero-worship was the strong Greek love of gossip and scandal. The Greeks loved to talk and exchange rumours in the *agora* (market place) in every *polis* and at leisurely *symposia* (dinner parties). At times they wrote down this gossip. This helps make the Greeks among the first true individuals in human history.

Left: Greek vases often depict aspects of everyday life, as in this scene of masters and pupils writing or playing the flute.

PERICLES: THE SUPREME DEMOCRAT c.495–429BC

Above: Aspasia, Pericles' mistress for many years, attended symposia *and talked to philosophers, which was most unusual for any woman in Athens. Highly intelligent, she bore Pericles a son who after Pericles' death was legitimized as an Athenian citizen, also a rare honour.*

Few elected politicians give their name to an age. None can match Pericles, whose name is synonymous with Athens' most brilliant decades. An Alcmaeonid by birth (he was Cleisthenes' great-nephew), Pericles was a visionary democrat by conviction, dominating Athenian politics for 30 years (460–429BC). Abraham Lincoln modelled his Gettysburg address on Pericles' funeral oration of 431BC.

Pericles entered public life by sponsoring Aeschylus' *The Persians* in 472BC. Unusually, this play dealt with recent events, praising Athenian democracy and its role in the Persian Wars. Both were policies of Themistocles, who was ostracized soon after. Pericles then joined forces with Ephialtes, a noted radical. In 462BC they persuaded the Assembly to transfer most remaining powers from the Areopagus to the Assembly or *Heliaea* (jury court). This marked Athens' transition to full democracy. After Ephialtes'

ANAXAGORAS

Pericles spoke only rarely in public so that people did not grow tired of his voice. But when he did, he was the greatest orator of his day, with a "nobility in his speech utterly free of vulgar mob-oratory", according to Plutarch. Pericles had learned his skills partly from Anaxagoras of Clazomenae. This philosopher so impressed contemporaries that he was nicknamed 'Brain Personified'. Anaxagoras questioned conventional wisdoms. Solar eclipses, for example, were natural phenomena, not signs from the gods. This was intellectually too daring even for Athens, however, and Anaxagoras had to flee the city in 428BC, accused of impiety.

murder by enraged opponents, Pericles became the radicals' leader, though still only in his thirties.

Pericles introduced modest payment for jurors and Council members – just enough to ensure that poverty stopped no Athenian from attending them. During subsequent wars he proved a competent *strategos*. After the Peace of Callias in 449BC ended the Persian Wars, Pericles urged that surplus public money be used to rebuild the temples on the Acropolis, whose blackened ruins had been left as sharp reminders of the Persian occupation. But this was a controversial use of tribute from allied states, and some Athenians, led by Thucydides son of Melesias, attacked him for it. Pericles, who exalted Athens' role as the educator of Greece,

Left: The Temple of Athena Nike (Victorious), although finished in 425BC after Pericles' death, derived from his vision of Athens as the 'school of Hellas', a beacon of democracy.

won the argument, and Thucydides was later ostracized. Athens under Pericles was, Thucydides the historian wrote, "ostensibly a democracy but actually ruled by one man". But, despite his "high note of aristocratic, even regal leadership" in Plutarch's words, Pericles remained accountable to the Assembly.

ARCHITECTURAL PATRON

Pericles' role in the building of the Parthenon, one of the world's most sublime buildings, alone would ensure his fame. He arranged for Ictinus and Callicrates to design the temple and Pheidias its superb frieze. He saw the project through to swift completion, gaining a name for financial probity, then rare. He also oversaw the building of the Odeon, a covered theatre where plays were previewed, and encouraged Herodotus to read aloud from his *Histories*, the world's very first.

WAR AIMS

Pericles was an imperialist, crushing the revolt of Samos in 440–439BC, for example. He was elected *strategos* every year from 443 to 430BC, heading the Board of Generals with increasingly

professional ease. Pericles probably felt that the Athenian Empire benefited all Greece, sheltering it from Persian power, encouraging democracy and, by keeping down piracy, boosting trade. Certainly Athens thrived, with Piraeus becoming the eastern Mediterranean's greatest port. But such open imperialism created many enemies. In 433BC Pericles claimed that he could see war "bearing down from the Peloponnese". How far his policies provoked that war remains debatable.

In the Peloponnesian War that started in 431BC, Pericles' overall strategy – retreat behind the Long Walls, let the Spartans ravage Attica, but maintain naval superiority – was approved by the Assembly. When plague hit the city in 430BC, however, the people turned on him and falsely fined him for speculation. He was reinstated only just before his death from after-effects of the plague in autumn 429BC.

Pericles married and divorced when young. Divorce was common in Athens, but it was customary to marry again. Pericles did not, preferring the company of his mistress Aspasia; he was exclusively heterosexual, unlike many Greeks. He cultivated a lofty dignity in both public and private life, restricting his social life as he grew busier. The poet Ion of Chios found him "insolent and conceited", but perhaps caught him on a bad day. He is always portrayed with a helmet because, his enemies said, he wanted to hide his odd-shaped head. He seems to have had no other obvious vices. His deathbed statement that "no Athenian ever put on mourning because of me" (i.e. his policies produced no needless casualties) may be questionable, but his place as Athens' greatest leader is not.

Left: Pericles' vision of a democracy that raises its citizens up, rather than dumbs them down, inspired later democrats such as American President Abraham Lincoln, who modelled his Gettysburg Address on Pericles' famous Funeral Oration of 431BC.

Below: The archetypal picture of Pericles in his helmet, which he would have worn as strategos (elected general). He often wore it on other occasions too – to hide the odd shape of his head, according to his enemies.

DEMOCRATS IN DEFEAT
ALCIBIADES AND DEMOSTHENES

Below: Demosthenes, orator, politician and attempted saviour of Athenian independence from Macedonia's rising power, is shown here with a scroll.

Although no two men were less alike than Alcibiades and Demosthenes, both ended their lives in exile and failure after early successes.

ALCIBIADES, *c.*450–404BC

The last Alcmaeonid to lead Athens, and almost the last aristocrat in politics, Alcibiades had a dangerous Byronic glamour. Related to Pericles, whose ward he became on his father's death in 447BC, he was notably handsome and self-willed. As a boy, when defeated in a wrestling match, he sank his teeth into his opponent's arm. Accused of fighting like a girl, he replied that he was biting like a lion. Throughout his life, he ignored all the rules.

COMMAND AND DESERTION

Alcibiades met Socrates when they were fellow soldiers at Potidaea in 430BC. The philosopher saved Alcibiades' life – a favour Alcibiades returned six years later at Delium – and tried to guide the gifted young man towards philosophical virtue. This was in vain, for Alcibiades, while flattered by Socrates' attentions (in Plato's *Symposium* he is shown trying to seduce the older man), was interested in fame and power. He cut off the tail of his dog so that everyone would comment on its state, and trailed a long purple cloak around the Agora. But when his chariot won first prize in the Olympic Games, and two others belonging to him came second *and* fourth, he could claim a truly Homeric victory. Athens loved him for it.

Standing for election as *strategos* in 420BC, Alcibiades faced little competition from Nicias, the timid conservative leader, or Hyperbolus, a radical and noted windbag. As *strategos*, Alcibiades created an anti-Spartan alliance in the Peloponnese. Not re-elected – which helped to lead to allied defeat at Mantinea – he looked elsewhere for glory, notably to Sicily,

Below: Alcibiades enjoyed a strange second career as an adviser in Sparta after being exiled. Sparta, although notoriously austere and lacking appeal for a sybaritic nobleman, boasted some fine temples, as these ruins reveal.

which was alluringly rich. Alcibiades urged an expedition there, finally with success. But he had made enemies by his arrogance and his scandalous friends who mocked the city's gods. When the herms (good-luck statues set around Athens) were found mutilated, he was accused of sacrilege. Denied a chance to clear his name, he sailed with the Syracusan expedition in 415BC but was recalled to face fresh charges. Escaping his captors, he reached Sparta. There he charmed his hosts and gave them excellent advice: invade Attica again and occupy the fort of Deceleia permanently. This devastated Athenian farming and mining.

Alcibiades' lack of patriotism was common among Greeks. But when he seduced the wife of King Agis, he had to leave Sparta fast. He crossed to Asia and persuaded Tissaphernes, a Persian satrap, that he could make Athens Persia's ally. The Athenians now wanted him back. As Aristophanes wrote, "they long for him, hate him and cannot do without him". Elected *strategos* by the fleet at Samos, he recaptured important cities on the Bosphorus in 408BC. He returned to Athens in seeming triumph in 407BC, but, when his helmsman Antiochus lost a pointless battle, he slipped away to his Hellespontine fort in disgrace. From it he rode out to warn the Athenian fleet about its dangerous position at Aegospotami – in vain. He was killed by assassins in Persian pay, who surprised him in bed with his last mistress, Timandra. She buried her lover, the last Alcmaeonid, in a foreign field.

DEMOSTHENES, 384–322BC

The finest of all Greek orators, Demosthenes was the last great Athenian democrat, who battled to save his city from foreign domination. Although he ultimately failed, his was a noble failure.

Orphaned when young, Demosthenes saw his guardians steal his inheritance and had to fight to regain it. A bookish, unathletic boy, he cured a stammer to become a superb professional speech-writer, the equivalent today of a barrister. Athens remained the foremost Greek

naval state, with interests around the Aegean. This led her to clash with Macedonia, rising fast under its ambitious new king Philip II. Demosthenes, realizing that Athens' independence could not survive Macedonian hegemony, became leader of the anti-appeasement party in Athens. To rouse his countrymen, who preferred to employ mercenaries rather than fight themselves, he made four fiery speeches: the *Philippics* ('against Philip'). In these, he urged resistance to Philip's promises and threats.

Demosthenes' great political achievement was the alliance with Thebes, Athens' old rival, against Macedonia in 338BC. He fought as a citizen-hoplite in the Battle of Chaeronea, but this proved Philip's greatest victory. Philip, who wanted Athens' fleet for his planned war on Persia, dealt with Athens gently. Later, while Alexander was conquering Asia, Demosthenes defeated Aeschines, his main Athenian enemy in a brilliant speech, *De Corona* (On the Crown), defending his right to honours for services to his city. After Athenian democracy was finally crushed by Macedonia in 322BC, Demosthenes killed himself rather than fall into Macedonian hands.

Above: Alcibiades counted among his friends the penniless philosopher Socrates, who had saved his life in battle in 430BC. Socrates discerned signs of greatness in the self-indulgent aristocrat, but Alcibiades disappointed his teacher by preferring worldly fame to areté *(virtue, excellence).*

Below: Demosthenes was a superbly rousing orator, but his words proved useless against Macedonian revolt.

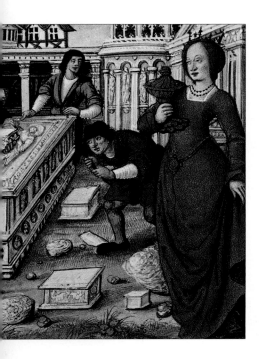

Above: A fanciful medieval portrayal of Artemisia, the fighting queen of Halicarnassus.

EXCEPTIONAL GREEK WOMEN
ARTEMISIA, OLYMPIAS AND ASPASIA

Women in classical Greece proper played no role in public life. But in Ionia and Macedonia, where they had more freedom than in Athens, some remarkable women emerged.

ARTEMISIA OF HALICARNASSUS, ACTIVE *c.*480BC

Artemisia, queen of Halicarnassus (today Bodrum) in Caria, was an exceptional queen. She took part in Xerxes' invasion of Greece, giving him unusually forthright advice. Her father, King Lygdamis, was Carian, but her mother was a Cretan aristocrat. Widowed young, Artemisia stepped into her unknown husband's royal shoes and ruled the city even after her son grew up.

She supplied five galleys to the Persian fleet in 480BC – Herodotus thought them the best ships after Sidon's – commanding them in battles off Euboea. When Xerxes held a council of war before the battle of Salamis, she alone advised against attacking the Greek fleet, saying that the Greeks could not stay long on the small, crowded island. Her advice was not taken and the Persians advanced to their defeat. In their rout, Artemisia's galley, chased by an Athenian trireme, rammed a Calyndian ship that was on her side but in her way. The Athenian trireme, thinking that Artemisia's ship was an ally, abandoned its pursuit. Artemisia saved her life by this quick thinking and gained kudos with Xerxes, watching from his shoreside throne. Thinking she had actually rammed a Greek ship, the King exclaimed: "My men are fighting like women and my women like men!"

ASPASIA, MISTRESS OF PERICLES

Aspasia came from Miletus, the most sophisticated city in the Greek world until its sack by the Persians in 493BC.

Like many adventurous Ionians after 480BC, she migrated west to Athens in search of her fortune. She became Pericles' mistress at about the time he became Athens' effective leader *c.*450BC, their relationship lasting until his death in 429BC.

She must have been highly intelligent as well as attractive, for Pericles' circle included the greatest minds of the age. Reputedly, she joined in discussions with the philosophers Protagoras and Anaxagoras, unlike a normal Athenian wife. (Significantly, we do not even know the name of Pericles' wife, whom he divorced.)

Aspasia's son Pericles, unlike Pericles' legitimate sons, inherited some of his father's talents as well as his name. Aspasia must also have helped to bring up Alcibiades, Pericles' brilliant but troublesome ward.

Right: This Roman-era portrait bust of Aspasia, Pericles' mistress, captures the intelligence, independence and noble beauty of the great statesman's lover.

Her relationship with Pericles fed slanderous gossip. He was depicted on stage as being in her power, although this was clearly not true. She was, however, caught up in the attacks on Pericles after plague broke out in 430BC and accused of impiety, according to Plutarch. After Pericles' death, however, her son Pericles was legitimized and granted Athenian citizenship, which was a rare honour. Aspasia then married Lysicles, a wealthy politician. She may have had the luck to die before 406BC, when her son was one of the six *strategoi* unjustly condemned to death for abandoning drowning sailors after the Battle of Arginusae.

OLYMPIAS, MOTHER OF ALEXANDER, *c.*364–316BC

Even wilder than Macedonia, Epirus, on the north-western edge of Greece, was ruled by kings who claimed descent from Achilles, greatest of Homeric heroes. Olympias, daughter of King Neoptolemus, reputedly met Philip of Macedonia at the mysteries (initiation into the religious ceremonies) on the island of Samothrace and fell in love. More probably their marriage in 357BC was arranged for political motives, as Philip covered his back (literally) with marital ties.

The birth of Alexander a year later produced the essential male heir, but the marriage was unhappy. Olympias was a tempestuous character, whose wrath could rival that of Achilles. Often ignored by Philip – who had mistresses, boyfriends and six other wives – Olympias turned to religion. She took part in the Bacchic mysteries, kept a sacred snake in her bed and sacrificed thousands of animals. She helped to choose her son's first two tutors and probably encouraged his belief that a god, not Philip, was his real father. Alexander inherited her fiery temper and supported her when she left Macedonia, enraged by Philip's last marriage to Eurydice. But he was reconciled with Philip, while she was divorced by him, returning only after Philip's murder in 336BC.

Olympias honoured the corpse of the assassin Pausanias, which suggests complicity in the murder, and had Eurydice killed. Alexander left her as queen in Macedonia when he crossed to Asia, but she quarrelled repeatedly with Antipater, his general. Hearing this, Alexander exclaimed that his mother charged him dearly for nine-months' lodging in her womb. In the long wars after Alexander's death, she retreated to Epirus, then returned to kill the half-witted King Philip III in 317BC. Besieged in Pydna herself a year later, she was starved into surrender. Macedonian soldiers sent to execute her refused "out of respect for her royal rank", so relatives of her victims finally killed her.

Left: Olympias, wife of Philip II of Macedonia and mother of Alexander the Great, was a passionate, fiery woman who frequently quarrelled with her husband. After her son's death she played a major role in Macedonian dynastic politics.

Below: Although classical Athens was an intensely masculine society, the city revered a female deity, Athena Parthenos, the warrior-goddess whose cult image was carried aloft in every Pan-Athenaic Festival. This statue is a copy of Pheidias' lost masterpiece.

EXTRAORDINARY SPARTANS
CLEOMONES AND BRASIDAS

Above: The agora of the ancient city of Sparta, home of one of the most absolute military regimes the world has ever known.

Below: David's famous depiction in 1814 of Leonidas, who with his Spartans fought the Persians to the last man at Thermopylae in 480BC, typifying Spartan bravery and military competence. But a more imaginative general such as Cleomones or Brasidas with 7,000 allied troops might have held the pass indefinitely.

Although the Spartan system discouraged individuality, some kings or generals escaped the general levelling, if at considerable personal risk.

CLEOMONES I: SPARTA'S DYNAMIC KING, REIGNED c.520–c.490BC

Even Cleomones' birth was controversial. His father, King Anaxandridas, had taken a second wife after his first failed to have children, but he kept her too. His second wife duly gave birth to Cleomones, but other boys were born soon after to the king's first wife.

Cleomones, succeeding to the throne c.520BC, soon showed unSpartan cunning. The tiny city of Plataea in 519BC asked for Sparta's protection against her powerful neighbour Thebes. Cleomones suggested that Athens, much closer, would be a better ally, thus embroiling Athens, still friendly to Sparta, with Thebes. The two cities' resulting enmity suited Sparta. In 510BC Cleomones led a Spartan army to expel Hippias from Athens, for the Delphic Oracle had

urged the Spartans to free the city. Cleomones probably knew that Cleisthenes, the Alcmaeonid, had bribed the Oracle, but he did not expect the subsequent democratic revolution. Marching back to Athens to support his aristocratic friend Isagoras, Cleomones was besieged on the Acropolis and had to bargain with the Athenian *demos* for his freedom – a humiliation for a Spartan king, which deepened when his avenging invasion of Attica collapsed in 506BC due to divisions in the army.

Cleomones' position after such a defeat may have been shaky in Sparta – he had envious half-brothers – but he ignored Ionian appeals for help against Persia in order to concentrate on Sparta's real enemy: Argos.

In a brilliant ruse in 494BC, Cleomones attacked the Argives during lunch, when they were not expecting it. After the defeated Argives took shelter in a sacred wood, he had it burnt down, killing 6,000 and crippling Argos for a generation. Cleomones may not have helped Ionia, but he still pursued a vigorous anti-Persian policy. The Athenian defeat of Persia at Marathon was partly due to his pressure on Athens' enemy Aegina to stop it 'medizing' (collaborating with Persia).

Cleomones fell from power c.490BC in mysterious circumstances after his part in bribing the Delphic Oracle to help depose Demaratus, his fellow-king, had been exposed. This encouraged his radical ideas about becoming sole king of a broader-based state than Sparta. For support he appealed to the Arcadians, Spartan allies in the Peloponnese. His scheme failed, he was deposed and declared mad. Locked up, he was said to have committed suicide, but was almost certainly killed. Sparta thus lost an unusually dynamic king.

BRASIDAS: A SPARTAN BY MISTAKE, DIED 422BC

Brasidas had so many non-Spartan qualities – flexibility, diplomacy, eloquence – that he should really be considered a Spartan by mistake. An officer's son, he grew up brave and tough but also able to think for himself, lacking the characteristic Spartan arrogance. Brasidas came to prominence in 431BC when he rescued Methone in the Peloponnese from an Athenian sea-borne attack with only 100 hoplites. He received an official award for this. He was less successful in 429BC in western Greece, for the Athenian fleet was vastly superior to the Peloponnesian.

But he shone again at the Spartan attack on Pylos in 425BC, when he urged on hesitant Spartans landing on the rocky shore. Badly wounded disembarking, he took no further part in what became Sparta's most shameful defeat.

His real opportunity came in 424BC, when Perdiccas of Macedonia and some northern cities appealed to Sparta for aid against Athens, wanting Brasidas as the general. Sparta would not risk Spartiates (soldiers from the ruling class) so far north but let Brasidas recruit 700 *helots* (slaves), whom he armed as hoplites. Picking up 1,000 allied mercenaries as he went, he saved Megara from Athenian attack. Marching swiftly through a hostile Thessaly, he reached Acanthus in the Chalcidice. This, like many Greek cities, was divided. Most Acanthians were content as Athens' allies, but they let Brasidas talk to them. He was so persuasive, promising to respect their liberties, that they went over to Sparta's side. Thucydides noted they were also worried about their grape harvest, with Brasidas' troops camped in their vineyards. Two other cities, Stagira and Argilus, joined on similar terms.

Then Brasidas had his greatest success, marching through the winter night to capture the unguarded bridge over the River Strymon. Beyond it lay Amphipolis, hugely important to Athens. Here again Brasidas triumphed by his oratory, offering such easy terms that the city

surrendered, unaware that Athenian *strategos* Thucydides was belatedly hurrying to their rescue. History's gain was Athens' loss, for she never recaptured Amphipolis. Brasidas had further successes through combined diplomacy and generalship, skilfully keeping his mixed army of mercenaries and ex-*helots* in fighting form. He was killed in battle at Amphipolis in 422BC leading a charge against Athenians attacking the city. With him died Sparta's most remarkable general.

Above: These hoplites and chariot from Laconia, c.500BC, show characteristic Spartan toughness. Such an upbringing created brave foot soldiers, not adventurous generals, who remained a rarity.

Below: Sparta occupied the fertile Eurotas Valley beneath Mt Taygetus, some of the richest farmland in Greece.

CONTRASTING GENERALS
CIMON AND EPAMINONDAS

Above: Miltiades, who masterminded Athenian victory at Marathon over Persia in 490BC, was the father of Cimon, another great general.

While Cimon of Athens was a bluff aristocrat but an excellent soldier, Epaminondas of Thebes was a general of genius who briefly made his city hegemon of Greece.

CIMON OF ATHENS, c.508–449BC

Cimon was the son of Miltiades, architect of the victory at Marathon in 490BC, but his mother was descended from Thracian kings. Cimon lacked "any spark of Attic cleverness and eloquence" said Plutarch, yet gave "an impression of great nobility and candour". Miltiades had died in disgrace and debt, so Cimon's youth was impoverished. He long lived with his sister Elpinice, which fed malicious rumours of incest, until the rich Callias married her for love and paid off their debts. Cimon himself often fell in love with aristocratic women, including Isodice from the rival Alcmaeonids. He was also fond of drink and kept open house on his estate, where all were welcome.

In 480BC, as Persian forces approached Athens, Cimon led the young knights up the Acropolis to dedicate their bridles to Athena before taking up spears and shields to serve as marines, a timely gesture. He fought bravely at Salamis and with Aristides commanded the Athenian fleet in 478BC against the Persians. The allied commander was the Spartan Pausanias, but he behaved so outrageously – raping freeborn girls, dressing in Persian robes – that the Greeks turned to Athens for leadership. Cimon became commander of the Delian League fleet, often re-elected *strategos* and capturing Persian strongholds. He also retrieved the supposed bones of Theseus, Athens' legendary king, from Scyros. His finest triumph came in 467BC, when he led a fleet to defeat the Persians at the River Eurymedon, destroying 200 ships and its army. By then, with Themistocles ostracized, Cimon appeared supreme in Athens, but city politics was fickle.

In 464BC an earthquake hit Sparta, triggering a *helot* rising. In despair, Sparta appealed to Athens, still an ally, for help. Cimon led 4,000 hoplites into Messenia, but they were rudely dismissed by the Spartans, who distrusted democrats. Back in Athens, radicals exploited Cimon's absence to introduce political reforms. For opposing these, he was ostracized. When war broke out between Athens and the Peloponnesians, Cimon volunteered to fight as an ordinary hoplite at Tanagra in 457BC – in vain. After his ostracism ended in 451BC, however, he commanded the

Left: A 19th-century recreation of the sea Battle of Salamis in 480BC, in which Cimon took part.

fleet that sailed against Cyprus. There he died, but his body was brought back in honour to Athens.

EPAMINONDAS OF THEBES
*c.*418–362BC

Epaminondas was Thebes' greatest general and statesman, who raised it briefly to hegemony in Greece and freed the *helots* of Messenia from Spartan oppression. The son of an impoverished noble, he studied under Lysis, the last Pythagorean philosopher. Epaminondas always led a life of almost ascetic poverty, refusing all gifts and bribes.

Thebes had been Sparta's keen ally against Athens in the Peloponnesian War but Spartan postwar arrogance drove it to ally with Athens in 395BC. In 382BC a Spartan coup installed a corrupt junta backed by a Spartan garrison in the Cadmaea, Thebes' citadel. Anti-Spartan feeling in the city grew until in 378BC a group of exiles returned. Disguised as prostitutes, they assassinated the junta's leaders and declared a democracy. Epaminondas and his friend Pelopidas now radically reorganized the Theban army. Instead of the usual eight-deep line of hoplites in the phalanx, with the best soldiers on the right, they raised the number to 50 deep on the left wing and trained it to attack at an angle. The core of this new army was the crack Sacred Band, 150 pairs of homosexual lovers bound by love and honour. Even Sparta's militarized pederasty had not produced this, but Epaminondas himself was unusual in never marrying and having only male lovers.

The new-model army proved its worth by crushing the Spartans at the Battle of Leuctra in 371BC, killing 400 Spartiates, a feat that astonished Greece. Soon the Thebans invaded the Peloponnese, liberating the Messenians from centuries of slavery. Epaminondas now revealed political as well as military genius. Messene was refounded as the *polis* of free Messenia, with imposing fortifications, and Megalopolis (big city) was founded

as a new capital for Arcadia, blocking Sparta's easiest egress north. Both cities were moderate democracies heading federations, like Thebes. Deprived of its *helot* serfs, Sparta sank forever to second-rank status. But Epamonindas could not establish a lasting peace. Athens, alarmed at Thebes' new power, allied with Sparta, and war continued. Epamonindas died in 362BC at the Battle of Mantinea fought against a mixed alliance. Thebes' brief hegemony was ended, but he deserved the inscription on his statue that, through his efforts and vision, "Greece was free" at least in part.

Above: The Apadana Staircase in Persepolis, capital of the giant empire that Cimon grew up trained to fight. Temperamentally pro-Spartan, he thought Athens should solely attack Persia.

Below: Thebes' heart was the Cadmaea, a citadel dating back to the Bronze Age, in which these remants of Mycenaean walls survive.

THE FIRST HISTORIANS
HERODOTUS AND THUCYDIDES

Below: Thucydides took as his theme the long war between Athens and the Peloponnesians. Hoplites such as these bore the brunt of the land fighting.

Although there had long been royal and religious chroniclers, analytical history starts with the Greeks. The term *historia* (inquiry or research) was actually first used by Herodotus.

HERODOTUS, 'FATHER OF HISTORY', *c.*490–425BC

Herodotus came from Halicarnassus (today Bodrum), an Ionian city with a strong Carian element. It supplied ships for the Persian fleet in 480BC but later joined the League of Delos, so it stood midway between Asia and Greece culturally and politically. This was apposite, for Herodotus, almost alone among Greek writers, viewed non-Greeks with an inquisitive, sympathetic eye, free of racial prejudice. Probably due to political troubles, he moved to Athens *c.*446BC, where he recited part of his *Histories* in public, then a common practice. He was paid 10 talents at Pericles' instigation for this, a large sum. He probably ended his days in Thurii in southern Italy.

Little else is known of him, but, through his writings, the reader gets to know a genial, intelligent, often discursive but never boring man. For Herodotus was not only 'the father of history' but an insatiably curious polymath. His researches led him to visit Egypt, Babylonia, the Black Sea and other areas, collating tales, legends and often surprisingly accurate facts, geographical, cultural and historical, about the ancient world. These make up the long preamble to his grand theme: the Great War between the Greeks and Persians of 499–478BC.

Herodotus was often, in the best sense, non-judgemental. He records different versions of an event, leaving the reader to decide between them. He can be over-credulous, as when describing the gold-digging ants of India, but he can also be sceptical – sometimes unduly so, for he dismissed the reports of Phoenician sailors circumnavigating Africa from east to west that the sun shone on them from *the north*. He was unfair to some individuals such as Themistocles, who appears only late in his account of the

Above: The probing intelligence of Thucydides, greatest of Greek historians, emerges in this Roman copy of an original Greek bust.

Persian invasion of 480BC. This probably reflects the bias of his sources, which he may not have fully realized. Herodotus knew little about military matters, never having been a soldier. He also had no idea of numbers, giving the total figure for Xerxes' invasion force as 1,700,000 men – absurdly large. But he wrote in clear Ionic Greek, being one of the first great prose writers.

THUCYDIDES, *c.*457–400BC

Little more than a generation younger than Herodotus, Thucydides was very different as a man and as a writer. While the supernatural still figures in Herodotus' picturesque accounts, Thucydides ignores dreams and omens. He may have read or heard Herodotus' work but probably regarded it as more of a muddle than a model. His great theme was the calamitous war between the Peloponnesians and Athens, which he was uniquely qualified to record. "I made it a principle not to write down the first story I heard, nor even to accept my own overall impressions. Either I myself witnessed the events described or I heard them from eye-witnesses whose reports I checked as

carefully as possible," he wrote. He has been called the 'historian's historian' because his analytical approach and sparse prose can often seem dry compared to other writers, but underneath boil surprising passions.

Thucydides was an aristocrat, related to Cimon and to the Thucydides who was ostracized for opposing spending tribute money on the temples. He grew up a conservative democrat but keenly admired Pericles, whose radical days were over by then. Thucydides was elected *strategos* in 424BC, but his command proved disastrous: he failed to save Amphipolis, that jewel in the Athenian Empire's crown, arriving too late with reinforcements, although he held the small port of Eion. Court-martialled, he was exiled, but being defeated by a general such as Brasidas was no disgrace, many felt. In exile, Thucydides devoted himself to his *History*, a rigorous analysis of the causes as well as course of the Peloponnesian War. After 404BC and Athens' final defeat, he returned to his city and probably died suddenly, for his history breaks off abruptly in late 411BC.

Thucydides thought that Athenian politics degenerated after Pericles' death, as demagogues such as Cleon (as he saw the man who had pressed for his banishment) came to dominate the Assembly. But although he treated the ineffectual Nicias kindly because he was a rich conservative, he also discerned the visionary statesman in Themistocles, an earlier radical. He perhaps overstated the defensiveness of Pericles' strategy, but his military judgement is sound. He also had a marked philosophical streak, shown in his account of the debate over the attack on Melos in 416BC, where the Athenians argue that 'might is right'. He was an inspiration to later historians, but none matched his intellectual rigour or brilliance.

Above: Herodotus was born in Halicarnassus (Bodrum), a city on the Greek world's edge, which helped make him unusually broad-minded.

Below: Often known as the 'father of history', Herodotus's historiae (inquiries) are the first true histories.

LATER GREEK HISTORIANS
XENOPHON, POLYBIUS & PLUTARCH

Above: The philhellenic Roman emperor Hadrian (ruled AD117–138) favoured Plutarch and Arrian, giving both imperial office.

Below: In this medieval picture, the translated works of Xenophon are presented to the French king Louis XII (reigned 1498–1515), showing the lasting fame of the ancient historian.

Later Greek historians, writing of people long dead, often had no first-hand accounts but relied on earlier histories that have vanished. But Xenophon did experience the later Peloponnesian War and his Anabasis himself.

XENOPHON OF ATHENS, *c.*430–354BC
The historian Xenophon was evidently always attracted to strong characters: first to Socrates, then the Persian prince Cyrus, and lastly Sparta's King Agesilaus. Born in Athens, Xenophon joined Socrates' circle, but it is doubtful how much of his philosophy he understood. His *Apology* defends Socrates so successfully that it seems bizarre that the philosopher was ever prosecuted for 'impiety'.

Xenophon left Athens soon after its defeat to make his fortune as a mercenary. He joined 'The 10,000' Greek hoplites whom Cyrus recruited to overthrow his brother Artaxerxes, the Great King. Xenophon immortalized their adventures in *Anabasis*, a gripping tale of the 'march upcountry' towards Babylon and their retreat under his leadership in 399BC after Cyrus' death. Xenophon reveals his generalship but conceals his enrichment from the campaign.

Returning to Greece, he settled in Sparta on a large estate given him by Agesilaus – a revealing choice. His most important historical work is his *Hellenica*, which continues Thucydides' account, starting "The next day…" and running to 362BC. Xenophon's account, while valuable, does not compare with Thucydides', especially in its later parts. In *Cyropaedia* (Boyhood of Cyrus) he gave a fictionalized account of the youth of Cyrus the Great, and also wrote on topics from horsemanship to housekeeping.

POLYBIUS, *c.*200–120BC
In the 2nd century BC Rome slowly, often brutally, took over the Greek world. By good fortune, the process found a perceptive, sympathetic historian in Polybius of Megalopolis in Arcadia. A general in the Achaean League, he was taken as a hostage to Rome in 167BC. There he met Scipio Aemilianus, one of Rome's great generals, becoming his friend and adviser on Greek affairs. He learnt Latin and came to admire Rome, seemingly still in its Republican prime. Permitted to travel, he visited Spain, Gaul and Africa. Allowed to return home in 150BC, he kept up links with Scipio, accompanying him to Carthage in the Third Punic War (149–146BC).

Polybius wrote the definitive history of Rome's rise to world power during 220–145BC in 40 books. He attempted to explain why this happened and to reconcile Greeks to Rome's new dominance by showing the excellence of its balanced

Above: Plutarch's Parallel Lives *(this is an edition of 1657) coupled 25 famous Romans with 25 famous Greeks, to demonstrate that there had once been Greek men of action and there were also Roman thinkers.*

constitution (in fact, already under growing strain). Although his style is turgid, his approach, as a former general and politician, is practical and intelligent, free of national prejudice. Most of his work survives only in paraphrases by later writers, but he deeply influenced Livy, the great Roman historian.

PLUTARCH, *c.*AD46–*c.*125

Born at Chaeronea in Boeotia, Plutarch is famous for his *Parallel Lives*, 50 biographies of paired-off famous Greeks and Romans. In them he aimed to show Greeks that Rome had produced more than just soldiers and to remind Romans that there had once been great Greek generals and statesmen. In his *Lives*, Plutarch too often accepted unreliable secondary sources as true, but his great gifts as a story-teller later influenced Renaissance writers such as Shakespeare.

Plutarch was more than just a biographer, however, being also a philosopher and a priest at Delphi and an active public citizen in Chaeronea. He was educated chiefly in Athens, where he became an adherent of Platonism. He also visited Rome several times, becoming a friend of the consul Sosius Senecio and ultimately of the philhellenic emperor Hadrian (AD117–138). The emperor made him governor of Achaea (south Greece) and gave him consular honours, but Plutarch remained devoted to his small home *polis*. Sadly aware that Greece's great days were past, one of his chief concerns was to restore the shrine at Delphi. Among his other works are a diatribe against Herodotus and his *Moralia*, essays attacking Stoicism and Epicureanism.

ARRIAN (FLAVIUS ARRIANUS), *c.*AD87–*c.*147

Arrian was an upper-class Greek, from Nicomedia in Bithynia (north-west Turkey), who lived at the zenith of the Roman Empire. His greatest achievement was to write a history of Alexander the Great that made intelligent use of primary sources such as Ptolemy and Aristobulus – officers who had served under Alexander but whose accounts have been lost. Arrian's eight-volume *Anabasis* (March Upcountry) survives, as does his *Indica*, a book about India based on accounts by Megasthenes of *c.*300BC and on the voyage made by Alexander's admiral Nearchus from the Indus. From Arrian we derive most of our knowledge of Alexander's life and character.

Arrian had a glittering career himself. His father was a Roman citizen, and he studied under Epictetus, the Stoic philosopher. Arrian rose to the highest office in the Roman state, becoming consul in AD129 (still an unusual honour for a Greek) under the emperor Hadrian, whose friend he was. He later was governor of Cappadocia (eastern Anatolia), commanding two legions with which he repelled an invasion by the Alans, a nomadic tribe from Central Asia.

Above: Plutarch, most prolific of ancient biographers, wrote 200 books in total. He was also a philosopher and priest.

Below: Sides of a gold coin of Alexander the Great, the subject of Arrian's great history, the book that gives us our definitive view of the world-conqueror.

PHILOSOPHERS IN POLITICS
THALES, EMPEDOCLES & DEMETRIUS

Early Greek philosophers were often closely involved in politics, for philosophy, a Greek invention, grew up in the streets and agoras of the *polis*, not in academic seclusion. This interaction had fruitful, sometimes surprising, results.

THALES, *c.*624–547BC

Greek philosophy was born in the Ionian port of Miletus, the largest and richest Greek city before 500BC, with Thales of Miletus, the very first philosopher. For Thales, philosophy meant *thinking* about every aspect of life, not quietly accepting old myths and legends. Speculating about the nature of the universe, he decided that water was the basic principle of everything, which was not so absurd for Greeks living by the sea. He learned enough about astronomy, possibly in part from Babylonia, to predict the eclipse of the sun in 585BC.

One day, he was walking along so lost in thought that he fell into a well and had to be rescued. Annoyed at becoming a laughing stock, Thales decided to get his own back. Shrewdly noting early indications that there would be a bumper olive harvest, he bought all the oil presses nearby and later charged his fellow Milesians extra to rent them, showing that philosophers could be practical too. Even shrewder was his suggestion that the Ionian cities, already threatened by powerful Asian monarchies, should form a league with its centre at Teos, a small, centrally sited city. Unfortunately, his advice was not taken and Ionia was conquered by Persia in 545BC.

EMPEDOCLES, *c.*495–*c.*432BC

Empedocles of Acragas was remarkably multi-talented. Not only philosopher and poet, he was also scientist, doctor and social reformer, a man of such visionary enthusiasm that some thought him a charlatan, others an almost divine hero. Both Aristotle and the Roman philosopher-poet Lucretius admired him, and it is only through their paraphrases of him that fragments of his work have survived.

In the 5th century BC Acragas (today Agrigento) was the richest city in Greek Sicily, as its splendid Doric temples show. Though born into its aristocracy, Empedocles was a radical democrat. He played a key role in overthrowing the tyrant Thrasydaeus in 471BC and establishing democracy in Acragas, which lasted until the Carthaginian attack in 406BC. He guided the city through its greatest period in a way comparable to

Below: A view of the Sicilian volcano Mt Etna erupting. Into its fiery heart Empedocles, the democratic statesman and mystical philosopher, threw himself, according to legend. More probably, he died peacefully in Olympia.

that of Pericles in Athens. He then retired in 445BC to travel. According to legend, he began proclaiming himself a god and committed suicide by throwing himself into the volcano of Mt Etna. More probably he died of natural causes in the Peloponnese, where his poems were recited at the Olympiad of 440BC.

As a philosopher Empedocles was among the most important pre-Socratic thinkers. He wrote a long poem, *On Nature*, of some 6,000 lines (only 350 of which survive) in which he propounded his general theory of the universe. He postulated four elements – earth, air, fire, water – governed by two opposed forces: Love, which attracts and unites, and Strife, which repels and divides. He realized that air was solid and suggested that light from the Sun must take some time to reach the Earth. This remarkably anticipates modern physics. All his science was tinged with mysticism, however, following the pattern set by Pythagoras, the pioneer of mystical mathematics.

DEMETRIUS, *c*.350–283BC
Plato had dreamt of a 'philosopher-king' ruling with supreme wisdom, but in the ten-year rule of Demetrius of Phalerum, Athens experienced almost the opposite. Demetrius might be called a rogue-philosopher, for he behaved outrageously, unlike any normal 'lover of wisdom' (which is what philosopher means).

A student of Aristotle but an Athenian citizen, Demetrius was installed in 317BC as a quisling ruler by Cassander, the Macedonian general ruling Greece. Demetrius' books on philosophy have

Above: The growing wealth of the Greek world, revealed in grand temples such as those at Acragas in Sicily, encouraged the development of philosophy.

been lost, only those on cooking, hairdressing and fashion surviving. This seems apposite for his strange regime. He reputedly organized processions led by a mechanical snail that spat saliva and accepted absurdly flattering epithets such as *lampito* (brilliant). Although it was a time of economic hardship, he gave wild parties and ordered 1,500 bronze statues raised in his honour. He was not brutal, but power lay with his Macedonian masters. When Cassander lost power and Demetrius was overthrown, the Athenians melted his statues down into chamber pots, now they were at last free to express their true feelings about him.

Below: The temple of Hercules at Acragas, one of the many fine temples erected in the 5th century BC, when Acragas was a flourishing democracy under the enlightened guidance of the polymathic Empedocles.

DEMETRIUS THE LIBRARIAN
Demetrius went on to advise Ptolemy I of Egypt about establishing the Library at Alexandria. With a reputed 500,000 volumes, it became the greatest library in the Ancient World. This suggests that Demetrius made a better librarian than philosopher-king.

CHAPTER VI

THE STRUGGLE FOR SUPREMACY

404–322 BC

With the end of the Peloponnesian War in 404 BC, an era of liberty seemed at hand. But this illusion was soon shattered. Sparta showed itself unfit to lead Greece, favouring corrupt despotisms. Spartan arrogance united former enemies, Athens allying with Corinth and Thebes and even Persia. The collapse of Spartan power after 371 BC saw Thebes as hegemon of Greece, but its achievements – spreading democracy, new forms of federalism – only worsened general instability. Men left home to fight as mercenaries while wars exhausted their own cities, leaving them prey to outside powers.

The first such power was Dionysius I, who created a vast Sicilian empire. Greece looked west in alarm, but Dionysius hardly interfered in its affairs and his empire soon collapsed. Jason of Pherae and Mausolus of Halicarnassus proved even more transitory as hegemons. Then a truly formidable power emerged: Macedonia. Philip II exploited Macedonian strength and Greek weakness to create a solidly based hegemony. At Corinth in 337 BC he declared a war of Panhellenic revenge against Persia. Alexander, his brilliant son, far exceeded his plans, so ending the Classical Age of Greece.

Left: The Temple of Apollo, Delphi, Greece's spiritual heart. Macedonia won Delphi, confirming its status as hegemon.

SPARTAN SUPREMACY
POWER AND CORRUPTION, 404–377BC

On Athens' surrender in April 404BC, Thebes and Corinth pressed for its total destruction. The Spartan commander Lysander refused, however, remembering Athens' glorious stand against Persia and aware that Athens, broken but still the largest Greek city, was a potential ally. At Athens Lysander installed an oligarchy, 'The Thirty Tyrants', backed by a Spartan garrison under a *harmost* (governor). The city, disarmed, became an ally of Sparta, as did most cities in its former empire, although the Thirty did not last long.

For smaller states, Lysander favoured *decarchies*: cliques of ten reactionaries eagerly wielding power long denied them. As Plutarch wrote: "In appointing these officials, Lysander simply handed out power to his cronies, giving them absolute powers of life and death." Backing each *decarchy* was a *harmost* and garrison. The tribute that had flowed into Athens was diverted to Sparta, but Sparta's former allies Thebes and Corinth gained nothing. This alienated them.

Below: The walls of Athens are pulled down to the sound of flutes after its final defeat in 404BC. This left the city nakedly vulnerable but, thanks to Lysander's intercession, Athens itself was spared destruction.

THE MARCH OF THE '10,000'

After the Peloponnesian Wars many Greeks, who knew only soldiering, were idle amid economic depression. In 404BC Cyrus, governor of western Asia, in rebellion against his brother Artaxerxes II, the new Persian king, required mercenaries. He hired c.10,000 Greek *hoplites*, who were seen as the world's best infantry, to boost his army. Well aware that Greeks would not march far from the sea, he claimed, on starting out in 401BC, to be fighting only Pisidian bandits inland.

Among the Greek officers was a bright young Athenian Xenophon. Marching ever further east, the Greeks grew restive when they realized that they had been misled. But they were induced by extra pay to keep going until they entered Babylonia (Iraq), then a fertile, exotic land.

At Cunaxa, Artaxerxes' army finally met his brother's. In the ensuing battle the Greeks were victorious but Cyrus was killed, leaving the Greeks lost in an alien empire. After the Persians murdered their generals in negotiations, the '10,000' chose as a new leader the persuasive Xenophon, who promised to lead them home. He kept his promise. They marched up through the unknown mountains of Kurdistan and Armenia, finally reaching the Black Sea at Trapezus, a Greek city (modern Trabizond), before turning for home.

Xenophon, a good writer as well as general, vividly recorded his adventure in *Anabasis* (March Upcountry). The Persian Empire's apparent vulnerability led many Greeks to dream of expansion east, with momentous later consequences.

TROUBLE AT HOME AND ABROAD

Although Sparta could now afford to maintain a fleet, the overall results were disastrous. On leaving their austere homeland, Spartans often became totally corrupt, and Spartan *harmosts* also became infamous for predatory sexual behaviour in Greek cities under their rule. Back home, Sparta's unique egalitarian system was undermined by its new wealth, since rich Spartans got richer, buying up land from poorer ones, who no longer qualified for Spartiate status. Sparta soon faced a shortage of Spartiates, the basis of its power, worsened by the relative freedom of its women, who preferred to marry richer Spartans. As a result, Sparta's birth-rate began to fall.

Sparta had supported Prince Cyrus' rebellion against his brother, King Artaxerxes II of Persia, but Cyrus was killed fighting at Cunaxa in 401BC. The Greek cities of Ionia, now free once more, appealed to Sparta for help against Persia, leading it into war with its former ally. The Spartan king Agesilaus, Lysander's protégé, led an army to Asia to attack Persia, gaining early successes. But, thanks to Persian gold, Athens began to revive, rebuilding its fleet. Lysander himself was killed in 395BC fighting at Thebes, which, like Corinth, had allied with Athens in the 'Corinthian War'. Documents found after Lysander's death revealed that he wanted to make Sparta's monarchy elective but more powerful, suiting Sparta's new imperial role.

In 394BC an Athenian fleet in Persian pay defeated the Spartans off Cnidus. This victory was countered by a bloody battle at Corinth when Spartan discipline crushed the armies of Thebes, Corinth and Athens. But when Athens rashly sent fleets to support anti-Persian rebels in Cyprus and Egypt, Sparta restored its ties with Persia, the new arbiter of Greece.

THE KING'S PEACE

Under the Persian King's Peace of 386BC, Sparta abandoned Cyprus and Ionia to Persia. The Peace theoretically guaranteed all European Greek cities' autonomy and forbade all confederations except Sparta's, considered a free alliance. This let Sparta destroy the Arcadian city of Mantinea, claiming that its existence violated the Peace, and move against a newly formed Chalcidic Confederacy.

En route north in 382BC, a Spartan army helped a pro-Spartan coup in Thebes. This action, actually breaking the Peace, marked the apogee of Spartan power. Three years later, a counter-coup led by Epaminondas ejected this regime, and Thebes allied with Athens. Spartan power was again threatened. Seven years later it would be crushed at Leuctra.

Above: Funerary stele of Democlides, an Athenian soldier killed at the Battle of Corinth in 394BC, when Spartan discipline managed to defeat the combined armies of Athens, Thebes and Corinth.

Below: The '10,000', the mercenary force led by Xenophon the Athenian, finally reach the Black Sea after a gruelling march through the Asian interior. They were jubilant at being back on the coast, so central to Greek life.

ATHENS: CRISIS AND RECOVERY 399-357BC

Above: The 4th century BC saw artists turn away from the severe heroism of the 5th century. Their new appreciation of female beauty is epitomized by the Aphrodite of Cnidus, one of Praxiteles' masterpieces.

Few cities appeared more defeated than Athens in 404BC, deprived of its empire, fleet, walls and democracy. But within a decade it had recovered, becoming once more a great naval power, albeit one chronically short of money. Even more swiftly, it regained its democracy, which worked smoothly until extinguished by Macedonian generals in 322BC.

'THE THIRTY TYRANTS'

Athens' defeat was welcomed by its oligarchs. Under Lysander's menacing eye, in July 404BC the Assembly voted power to 'The Thirty Tyrants'. The two leaders were the extremist Critias, one of Socrates' former students, and Theramenes, a moderate. They set up a body of the Eleven, ruthless special police. Only 3,000 citizens had civil rights; the rest were powerless. Leading democrats were killed in a reign of terror, as were moderates such as Niceratus, Nicias' son, and rich *metics* (foreign residents) such as Polemarchus. Athenians were ordered to arrest their fellow citizens, so implicating themselves in the regime's crimes. Most complied, but Socrates refused – and uniquely went unpunished.

Democrats fled to nearby states, whose feelings towards Sparta were changing fast. In December 404BC Thrasybulus, Anytus and 70 other exiles seized the fort of Phyle near the border. The junta's attempt to eject them failed due to a snowstorm, and they gained support. Alarmed, the oligarchs quarrelled, with Theramenes being killed as Critias took control. He appealed for Spartan help, and a garrison of 700 occupied the Acropolis. After another attempt in May 403BC to dislodge the democrats failed, Thrasybulus captured Piraeus. Critias, trying to retake it, was killed in the fighting.

Again the oligarchs appealed to Lysander, but King Pausanias, his bitter enemy, now intervened, changing Spartan policy. Pausanias let the oligarchs withdraw to Eleusis while Athens worked out a new settlement. By late 403BC, democracy had been restored with a general amnesty. Athens was free again.

Right: The stele of Dexileos, who was killed in 393BC, during the war against the Corinthians, and buried at the Kerameikos, a quarter built up in the age of Themistocles.

THE TRIAL OF SOCRATES

In 399BC Meletus, supported by Anytus, accused Socrates of "not believing in the city's gods, of introducing new gods … and corrupting the young". No court records exist of this most famous trial, but Socrates' followers Plato and Xenophon gave vivid descriptions, although neither was present. Meletus is unknown but Anytus was a democratic hero of Phyle. Socrates had fought bravely too, but was better known as an incessant questioner of customs: religious, social and political. Among his ex-students were Alcibiades, the traitor, and Critias, leader of 'The Thirty Tyrants' – odious connections. But, due to the amnesty, Socrates could not be attacked on political grounds.

A charge of impiety, however, was different. Religion in ancient Greece was a public affair: offend the gods and you risked your city suffering. The 501 jurors – chosen by lot to represent public opinion – must have seen Socrates arguing in the streets. Back in 423BC he had been caricatured in Aristophanes' play *The Clouds* as a Sophist smart alec, who taught the young about new, amoral gods. This made audiences laugh, but by 399BC many felt that Socrates' constant questioning was no laughing matter. Even so, the majority finding him guilty – 280 to 221 – was small. When he mockingly proposed public dinners as his punishment, the majority for the death penalty was larger, but he was expected to escape. Instead, he chose death. Martyr of philosophy or teacher of tyrants? Both are valid viewpoints, but Socrates was the *only* man executed for his beliefs in classical Athens.

Above: The trial of Socrates in 399BC was a seminal, still contentious event in Western intellectual history. In this 17th-century painting the philosopher, accused of corrupting the young and introducing new gods, kills himself by drinking hemlock, still debating with his followers.

THE SECOND CONFEDERACY

Although free, Athens was hardly prosperous, but it could draw on the gold of Persia, then hostile to Sparta. Athens was soon fighting Sparta, in 394BC allying with Corinth and Thebes. In 390BC Iphicrates, an innovatory *strategos*, defeated a Spartan force outside Corinth using *peltasts* (light-armed troops). With Persian money Athens had rebuilt its Long Walls by 393BC.

Refortified, Athens began trying to regain its empire, rashly helping Evagoras of Cyprus in revolt against Persia. This led to Spartan–Persian rapprochement in the 'King's Peace' of 386BC, reaffirming Spartan hegemony in Greece. Sparta's actions over the next years united Greece against it, however. After an attempted Spartan raid on Piraeus in 378BC, Athens allied with Thebes and formed a totally new naval confederacy of its own.

Aimed against Sparta, this tried to avoid the mistakes of the first confederacy by having a separate council for the allies that Athens could not dominate and forbidding *cleruchies* (settlements). Initially popular, with 70 states joining, its fleet defeated the Spartans at Naxos in 376BC. The *strategos* Timotheus sailed victoriously round the Peloponnese in 376BC, defeating the Spartans at Alyzia in 375BC. With further operations hampered by lack of money, however, the war dragged on.

Right: The new, almost languid sensuality of 4th-century art is apparent in Praxiteles' Hermes and the Infant Dionysus.

THEBES: A BRIEF HEGEMONY 377–362 BC

Above: The sphinx, the mythical creature connected through the Oedipus legend with Thebes. Its enigma in a way illustrates the Theban dilemma: freeing the Peloponnese from Spartan tyranny brought chaos, not democratic order.

Below: Epaminondas' novel tactic at Leuctra, when Sparta was for the first time defeated in open battle, was to increase the weight of his left wing, massing Theban hoplites 50 deep so that they punched through the weaker lines of their opponents.

In the winter of 379–378 BC the Spartan-backed junta in Thebes was overthrown in a dramatic coup. The plotters, led by Pelopidas, entered the junta's symposium one evening in drag as courtesans and killed them all. They then instituted a new democracy, which joined the second Athenian Confederacy. While Thebes repaired its defences against inevitable Spartan counter-attacks, Epaminondas and Pelopidas, both *polemarchs* (commanders), reorganized the Theban army, making it far more professional. They founded, or refounded, a crack corps, the Sacred Band: 150 pairs of lovers, mature men bound to each other by the strongest ties possible. Over the next 40 years they proved to be the best hoplites in Greece.

In 371 BC Athens and Sparta, tired of inconclusive warfare and worried about the rise of Thebes, signed the Peace of Callias. This reaffirmed the principle of each city's autonomy, as in the 'King's Peace' 15 years earlier, but the Spartan and Athenian leagues were specifically excluded. Theban control over Boeotia was not, however, for it was contentious.

(Thebes had recaptured Plataea to the east, whose citizens fled to Athens, while to the west Phocis, another old Athenian ally, was attacked. Thebes was therefore excluded from the peace.) Just weeks later, in July 371 BC, Sparta sent a Peloponnesian army under King Cleombrotus against Thebes, which had only one ally: Jason of Pherae in Thessaly.

BATTLE OF LEUCTRA

Cleombrotus, approaching Thebes from the south, found the Theban army drawn up at Leuctra. The Spartans, like everyone in Greece, expected to win, as they had won every set battle for 200 years. They probably had *c.*11,000 men, mostly allies, against *c.*7,000 Thebans. Cleombrotus with his crack troops was on the Spartan right, as usual. But Epaminondas put his best troops on his *left*, deepening the Theban phalanx from the usual 8–12 men to 50 – a vast increase in striking power. Although Sparta's slingers defeated the Thebans, the Theban cavalry worsted the Spartans. Then the Theban hoplite wedge crashed into the Spartan right, breaking it. Cleombrotus was killed, his army collapsing like dominoes. About 400 full Spartiates were killed – a huge loss – and Sparta's legendary invincibility was over.

The immediate consequences of the victory were muffled by Jason of Pherae, who rapidly marched south to Leuctra to impose a truce. The Spartans were allowed to evacuate Boeotia. But when Jason's power ended soon after with his assassination, Thebes became Greece's new hegemon. This alarmed Athens almost as much as Sparta.

THE PELOPONNESE SET FREE

As news of Sparta's unprecedented defeat – by *inferior numbers* – spread around Greece, states long subject to its heavy

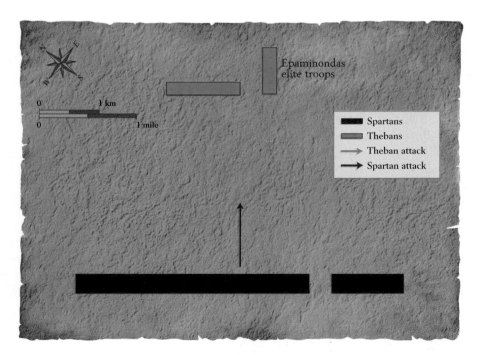

Epaminondas elite troops

■	Spartans
■	Thebans
→	Theban attack
→	Spartan attack

0 1 km

0 1 mile

Left: When Epaminondas led the Theban army into the Peloponnese in the winter of 370BC, he founded a huge new federal capital, Megalopolis, to which smaller settlements nearby, such as Bassae with its renowned temple, sent delegates.

rule began to revolt. Its loathed *harmosts* (governors) were thrown out, replaced by democracies. Among the first to revolt were the Mantineans of Arcadia, long denied a proper *polis* by Sparta. While their old city was rebuilt and rewalled, Mantinea helped form a Pan-Arcadian Federation with a new capital, Megalopolis (great city). Defended by double walls, it had a grand theatre, *agora*, temples and a federal army of 5,000 men.

Arcadia was a federal democracy, with most of its citizens having a vote. In 370BC revolution at Tegea led it to join Arcadia, but Tegea's exiled oligarchs appealed to Sparta. Arcadia in turn appealed to Athens, but, as Athens proved non-committal, it turned to Thebes. This was Epaminondas' chance.

FOUNDING MESSENE

In late 370BC a Theban army invaded the Peloponnese. Almost unopposed, it ravaged the long-inviolate territory around Sparta itself; the unwalled city seemed set to fall. But winter floods swelled the River Eurotas and the only bridge was strongly defended, so Epaminondas withdrew. This was a huge blow to Spartan pride, but worse followed. Epaminondas led his

army into Messenia, whose long-enslaved *helots* rose en masse. A new city of Messene was founded in 369BC on Mt Ithome, with splendid new walls 8km/ 5 miles long. Messenian exiles flocked back to their new *polis*, whose very existence doomed Spartan power. There were only 1,500 full Spartiates left anyway.

Athens, meanwhile, allied with Sparta. This was not so odd, for in the subsequent confused years states constantly changed sides. The Arcadians themselves did not want to swap Theban hegemony for Sparta's.

Pelopidas then led expeditions to Macedonia, trying to extend Thebes' influence north, while Dionysius (tyrant of Syracuse) and Persia intervened in Greek affairs, neither to much effect.

Epaminondas made four invasions of the Peloponnese, the last ending in his fatal victory at Mantinea in 362BC – fatal both to him, for he died of his wounds, and to Theban hopes of supremacy. With Pelopidas also dead, Thebes lacked great leaders. While it had finally ended centuries of Spartan supremacy and helped to free the Peloponnesians, Thebes' hegemony left Greece more exhausted and divided than ever.

Below: The massive walls of the Arcadian Gate in Messene, a city beneath Mount Ithome that Epaminondas founded in 369BC as a secure polis for Messenians who had been long enslaved by Sparta.

THE SYRACUSAN EMPIRE
411–337BC

When Syracuse defeated the Athenian invasion in 411BC, it was a democracy like Athens, as Thucydides noted, but a very unstable one. Hermocrates, leader of the defence, took 25 ships east to help Sparta, but radicals in the city then banished him. They also embroiled Syracuse in a war with Carthage, which had colonies in western Sicily. Called in by half-Greek Segesta against its rival Selinus, the Carthaginians landed with a huge army in 409BC. This captured Selinus and took Himera, another Greek city. Reputedly 3,000 Greek captives were sacrificed to Carthage's gods afterwards.

DIONYSIUS' GROWING POWER
Hermocrates was killed soon after while trying to re-enter Syracuse. Carthage then attacked Acragas, Sicily's richest city. Acragas' notoriously soft inhabitants – guards on night duty were limited to one mattress, two pillows and a quilt each – fled in panic in 406BC after a relief effort failed. As the Carthaginians besieged Gela, the next city along, panic grew in Syracuse too. Dionysius, one of Hermocrates' officers, accused the generals of treachery, becoming a *strategos* himself. In 405BC Syracusans voted him sole powers as *strategos autokrator* (supreme general) and a bodyguard of 1,000. With it, he made himself tyrant. His rule, a demagogic dictatorship but with rich backers, lasted until his death.

Dionysius' first campaign to save Gela in 405BC failed, and he had to abandon half of Greek Sicily to Carthage. Refugees streamed into Syracuse, swelling its population, as did deportees from Naxos (Taormina) and Catania – Greek cities that he had attacked without provocation. Dionysius made Ortygia, the old island core of the city, into his citadel, expelling from it all but 10,000 trusted mercenaries. Inside its turreted walls he survived a serious revolt in 403BC. Around Syracuse city he built the strongest walls yet seen, enclosing *c.*1,200ha/3,000 acres.

Meanwhile, he was planning revenge on Carthage, the excuse for his tyranny. Over the next years Syracuse rang to the sound of hammers and anvils. An army 80,000 strong, and a navy of 300 galleys – including the first quadriremes and quinqueremes, larger and more powerful than triremes – were assembled. Dionysius also developed the first siege engines to hurl heavy stones 300m/325 yards. Most Syracusans, whatever they felt about his tyranny, supported this armaments programme.

THE SIEGE OF MOTYA
With his base assured, in 397BC Dionysius renewed the war with Carthage. Marching to the far end of the island, he besieged the city of Motya. This was thought impregnable on its island, but Syracusan engineers built a causeway

Above: The ruins of Motya, the Carthaginian stronghold in western Sicily that Dionysius I besieged.

Below: The ruins of Carthage near modern Tunis. The perennial threat of this great enemy of the Greeks in Sicily was invoked by Dionysius I to justify his prolonged tyranny.

across the bay to let their siege-engines attack it. The battle was long and bitter. Even after their walls were breached, the Motyans fought back street by street, until a night attack finally crushed them. For the first time since 480BC, Greeks had captured a Carthaginian city. The resulting slaughter was terrible until Dionysius, mindful of the slave market, halted it.

COUNTER-ATTACK AND FURTHER CONQUESTS

Next year Himilco of Carthage, landing with an army, recaptured but did not rebuild ruined Motya, instead founding Lilybaeum nearby. Marching east, he founded on the site of Naxos a new city for the native Sicels, Taormina, later to be a Greek city. Himilco defeated the Syracusan fleet, but his attack on Syracuse itself met with disaster, thanks to its strong walls, an outbreak of plague in his army and a brilliant counter-attack by Dionysius. Dionysius let Himilco himself escape, but he had won the war. The peace treaty he made in 392BC was Machiavellian: the Carthaginians were restricted to the north-west of the island but not ejected, remaining a potential threat to justify his continued tyranny.

Master of Greek Sicily, Dionysius now turned to Italy. He had asked for a bride from Rhegium (Reggio) on the Straits of Messina, but was offered only their hangman's daughter, an unforgivable insult. In 391BC he duly attacked Rhegium. Initially defeated at sea, he waged war on the mainland with great success. He finally captured Rhegium after a long siege in 387BC, enslaving its citizens. He now controlled both sides of the Straits and much of southern Italy, the powerful city of Taras (Taranto) being his ally. Dionysius founded colonies up the Adriatic as far north as Hadria on the River Po, with trade flourishing in this new empire. After another war with Carthage, he had to cede Sicily west of the River Halcyus in 383BC. This still left him with most of the island, the greatest power in the Greek world, both feared and courted.

TYRANNY AND CULTURE

Dionysius liked to claim that he was not a tyrant, simply a *strategos* with exceptional powers. The Assembly continued to re-elect him – it had no option – and the city prospered as an imperial capital. But Syracusans were heavily taxed, under military rule and surrounded by barbarous newcomers. Dionysius himself, like many dictators, suffered from paranoia. He had visitors to his court strip-searched for weapons and allowed no one to shave him except his daughters.

Above: The Temple of Hercules in Acragas, the famously rich Greek city in western Sicily that fell without a fight to the Carthaginian advance in 406BC.

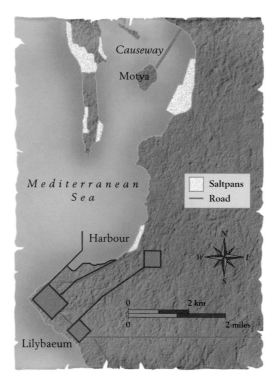

Left: Motya on its island was long considered impregnable. But Dionysius' engineers built a causeway out to it on which they brought up siege engines to take it in 397BC.

Above: The nymph Arethusa on a coin designed by Euanitos in the 4th century BC. Syracuse produced some of the most beautiful Greek coins that have ever been minted.

He did not even trust his wives – he had several simultaneously, for political reasons – but made them await him lying naked on a bare bed surrounded by water, so that he could see they had no daggers under the sheets. According to Plutarch, the tyrant hired prostitutes to spy on the citizens, executing 10,000 Syracusans as alleged traitors.

Dionysius harmed rather than helped Hellenism overall. He destroyed old Greek cities that opposed him, replacing their citizens with non-Greeks so that they no longer counted as true Hellenic *poleis*. But he admired Greek culture, inviting the hedonistic philosopher Aristippus, once a student of Socrates, to stay at his luxurious court. (The two men got on surprisingly well.) And Dionysius had literary ambitions himself, entering several contests.

In 367BC Athens, trying to woo him as an ally, awarded his *Ransom of Hector* first prize at the Lenaean festival. Overjoyed, Dionysius drank so much that he died. The Roman historian Cornelius Nepos acquitted Dionysius of a tyrant's three typical failings – lust, avarice and greed – but his empire rested wholly on force.

DION AND DIONYSIUS II

Dionysius I claimed to have left an "empire bound with steel", but the 29-year-old heir Dionysius II lacked his father's ruthlessness. He ended a war with Carthage, but a peaceful warlord risked seeming redundant, especially as he did not concentrate on ruling the empire. Instead, he swung between debauchery – he was excessively fond of wine and women – and philosophy, to which his relative Dion introduced him. Dion, an aristocrat who had married into the tyrant's family, meanwhile continued as chief minister.

Dion had once studied under Plato, the Athenian philosopher, and he persuaded the amenable young ruler to invite Plato to his court. Plato, already in his sixties, reluctantly agreed and made two visits to Syracuse, both of which turned out badly since Dionysius proved as idle a philosophy student as he was a ruler. Philistus, head of a rival faction, turned Dionysius against Dion, who went into exile in Athens.

Below: Part of the walls around Syracuse that Dionysius extended and strengthened to cover 1,200ha/3,000 acres, making his capital much the largest Greek city.

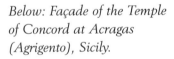

Below: Façade of the Temple of Concord at Acragas (Agrigento), Sicily.

PLATO AND THE PHILOSOPHER-KING

Although born into its ruling class, Plato turned his back on Athens' democratic politics after Socrates, his revered master, was put to death in 399BC. He spent years abroad, in Italy meeting Archytas, the Pythagorean philosopher-ruler of Taras. Visiting Sicily in 388BC, he fell foul of Dionysius I's paranoia. Arrested and deported, he was reputedly sold as a slave. Although soon rescued, it left him thinking tyranny even worse than democracy.

Plato now founded his Academy, the world's first university, outside Athens. In it a select few, including Dion, could study undisturbed. There Plato wrote *The Republic*, his blueprint for the ideal society ruled by an intellectual elite, but he did not envisage its realization on Earth. Yet when Dion begged to him to come and teach the young Dionysius II, he could hardly refuse. It was an unparalleled chance to educate this powerful ruler as a 'philosopher-king' guided by selfless wisdom of the truest kind.

Dionysius greeted Plato's arrival with delight. He dismissed his call-girls and fellow-boozers and began to study maths, which Plato thought essential for philosophy. But the young tyrant soon grew bored and, although he refused to let Plato leave, slipped back to his old ways. Finally allowed home, Plato returned to philosophy with relief. But in 357BC he was again invited, this time by Dionysius himself, who claimed to be studying philosophy seriously. Wearily, Plato again made the long voyage, only to find that the tyrant considered himself his equal as a philosopher. Plato was imprisoned and only freed because Archytas of Taras intervened. Back in Athens, he wrote *Laws*, his last and grimmest work on politics, effectively taking Sparta as his model.

Above: Plato the Athenian philosopher made three visits to Syracuse, the last two in the hope of turning its young ruler Dionysius II into a 'philosopher-king'. All ended in failure.

He returned to Sicily in 357BC with a tiny force, landing at Heraclea in the west. Marching on Syracuse, he was welcomed and seized the outer city, proclaiming the restoration of democracy. Dionysius, away in Italy, returned in time to save Ortygia. Murderous civil strife followed, Dionysius' Italian mercenaries slaughtering the citizens when they voted out Dion. Dion returned to save the city but ended becoming a tyrant himself, assassinated in 354BC.

TIMOLEON'S RESTORATION

A decade of civil war ravaged Sicily, numerous tyrants emerging only to be quickly murdered. Finally in 345BC Corinth, Syracuse's mother-city, sent out Timoleon, a man of exceptional integrity and ability. He drove out the tyrants and in 339BC defeated the Carthaginians, who had again attacked. Timoleon restored a limited democracy, re-peopling Syracuse with 60,000 new immigrants from old Greece. He retired universally honoured, dying in 337BC, but his settlement unravelled within a few years.

Right: Ortygia, the island core of Syracuse that Dionysius I made into his own citadel, expelling all citizens living there.

ABORTIVE EMPIRES
JASON AND MAUSOLUS, 375–353 BC

In 362 BC Theban victory at the Battle of Mantinea reconfirmed that Sparta could never regain her old position but left everything else more unsettled than before. Epaminondas' death at Mantinea had ended Thebes' brief hegemony, never fully accepted by most of Greece. By then, all the traditional main powers faced varying degrees of financial and political exhaustion. The resulting vacuum in Greek affairs began to pull in more powerful rulers from the Greek fringes. Two new powers emerged that seemed poised to dominate Greek politics, but both rapidly faded after their ruler's death.

JASON OF PHERAE
REIGNED 380–370 BC

Thessaly, the northernmost part of Greece proper, was unusually large and fertile – promising territory for any would-be dynast or ruler. With better-watered pastures than southern Greece, it supported superb cavalry on a scale unthinkable further south. But it had long remained divided between feuding aristocratic clans – all claiming descent from Hercules, like the kings of Sparta, the most notable being the Aleuads. Its coastal cities were intermittently independent. This disunity made Thessaly a pawn in the hands of outside powers, Persian, Athenian or Spartan. Xerxes had recruited its cavalry for his great invasion of 480 BC, but their 'medizing' did not undermine Thessaly's status as fully Greek. Although by the 4th century BC life based on the *polis* was spreading throughout Thessaly, it needed a leader of genius to unite it. In Jason, Thessaly briefly found one.

The ancient title *tagus* (lord) of Thessaly had long been awarded to a ruler who could unite the land. By 380 BC Jason, tyrant of Pherae in south-central Thessaly, was powerful enough to be hailed as *tagus* by other clans and cities. He began organizing a Thessalian army on a federal basis. By then he had also intervened in Euboea, if ineffectually, for Sparta opposed him. The Spartan outpost at Heraclea near Thermopylae blocked his way south into central Greece.

The news of Sparta's shocking defeat at Leuctra by Thebes in July 371 BC gave Jason his opening. He raced south with his cavalry, moving so fast through hostile Phocis that it could not stop him, and reached Boeotia in time to act as armed arbitrator. The Thebans had to let the Spartans, still numerically the larger army, return to the Peloponnese. Jason did not want an over-mighty Thebes. On his way home he demolished the fortress of Heraclea, opening the way into Greece.

Jason's army, composed of Thessalian cavalry and mercenary infantry, was now the strongest in Greece, and he began building a navy. He seemed the new Greek hegemon and talked of a Panhellenic war against Persia. He aimed to dominate the next Pythian festival at

Above: The fertile plains of Thessaly, here seen from the rocks of Meteora, provided good pasture for Jason's excellent cavalry.

Below: The island, now peninsula, in Halicarnassus (modern Bodrum) on which Mausolus built his citadel with a double harbour for his growing fleet in c.360 BC.

Left: After Mausolus' sudden death in 353BC, his widow built him a grand tomb adorned with works by Greek sculptors. It later became one of the Seven Wonders of the World and gave us our modern word 'mausoleum'.

Below: The dramatic features of Mausolus, dynast of Caria, who broke free of Persian overlordship to create his own empire that for a time seemed to threaten Greece.

Delphi, one of the greatest in the calendar, and to become President of the Amphictyonic Council controlling Delphi. But one day, late in 370BC, as he was reviewing his cavalry he was assassinated by some Thessalian nobles for personal reasons. His son Alexander succeeded him as *tagus* but lacked his ability. Alexander was defeated by Thebes in 364BC, although that victory cost the Theban general Pelopidas his life. Alexander lived on until 358BC, his powers much reduced.

MAUSOLUS OF CARIA
RULED 377–353BC

In the 4th century BC the Persian Empire's westernmost satraps in Asia Minor gained increasing powers that made them, if not independent, in practice far more powerful, even able to pass on their titles to their heirs. Several joined the 'Revolt of the Satraps' in the 360s BC, which shook the empire. Of these dynasts, Mausolus, who succeeded his father as satrap of Caria in south-west Asia Minor in 377BC, was the most powerful. He moved his capital from inland Mylasa

down to Halicarnassus, where he ruled with half-Hellenic, half-Carian splendour. He built himself a castle on the island (now peninsula) outside Halicarnassus and a double harbour for the city.

Now established, he began to expand his power: south-east toward Lycia, north toward Miletus and, most significantly, west over the islands. This meant a clash with Athens. The Second Confederacy in Athens was proving increasingly unpopular, as she reneged on initial promises not to exploit her allies, planting *cleruchs* (colonists) in Samos again, for example. In 357BC, when Chios, Cos and Rhodes revolted in the so-called 'Social War', they looked to Mausolus for support. He shrewdly let these Greek cities govern themselves, providing only small garrisons. But his mini-empire came to nothing, for he died suddenly in 353BC, after which his widow Artemisia ruled.

To commemorate her husband, she built his tomb, the Mausoleum, at Halicarnassus, which became one of the Seven Wonders of the World. Its magnificence displayed the dynasty's wealth and gave us the word 'mausoleum'.

THE 'SACRED WAR'
357–346 BC

Above: Delphi was sacred to Apollo, here seen in relaxed mode playing with a lizard, in a sculpture by Praxiteles.

Delphi was the holiest place in the Greek world, sacred to the god Apollo. For centuries cities across the Greek world, besides non-Greek kingdoms such as Lydia, had enriched the shrine with temples and statues. Set in a cleft in the mountains, Delphi itself was a tiny, powerless *polis*. Its accumulated wealth relied for protection less on awe of the god, real though that was, than on the Amphictyonic Council, backed by general Greek support. 'Sacred Wars' arose when states contested control of the shrine. The most significant resulted from Thebes' renewed attempts to dominate her immediate neighbours. It paved the way for Macedonia's domination.

PHOCIS SEIZES DELPHI

In 357 BC the Theban-dominated Amphictyonic Council fined the little state of Phocis for "cultivating sacred ground", which was an excuse for letting Thebes attack. As expected, Phocis would (or could) not pay the massive fine. Unexpectedly, their leader Philomelus seized Delphi early in 356 BC and 'borrowed' Delphic gold to hire a mercenary army of 5,000 men. He won Spartan and even Athenian tacit approval if not active support, but killed himself after having been defeated by the Thebans in 354 BC.

Thebes, thinking the war over, hired out many of its best troops to a Persian satrap, but Onomarchus (Philomelus' successor) took over the tattered Phocian army. He helped himself to more of Apollo's money, made alliances, with Pherae among other places, and recruited fresh troops. With these he won a series of startling victories, defeating Philip II of Macedonia in Thessaly in 353 BC.

At this stage Phocis ruled most of central Greece, but Philip, returning with a larger army, drove the Phocians from Thessaly in 352 BC. When Athens sent a force to hold Thermopylae, however, Philip prudently retreated to Thessaly, for the moment not wishing to offend Athens, still the greatest Greek city.

MACEDONIA'S VICTORY

The power of Phocis relied totally on Delphic money to pay its mercenaries. As this ran out, its fortunes began to decline, hastened by internal divisions. Onomarchus, killed in battle, was replaced by Phalaecus, who was soon dismissed (in theory, though in practice he still held Thermopylae, the gates of Greece). Both Athens and Sparta were

Left: The Tholos of the temple to Athena Pronoia built in Delphi, c.390 BC. Delphi was filled with sacred treasures. Melted down, these paid for a large mercenary army, so briefly making tiny Phocis hegemon of Greece.

Right: Consulting the Delphic Oracle. The god spoke to supplicants through his priestess the Pythia, who sat, probably drugged, on a stool over a chasm. Delphi's utterances were notoriously ambiguous.

preoccupied with events elsewhere when Thebes appealed to Philip for help against Phocian troops ravaging its borders. Philip moved swiftly south, Phalaecus surrendering Thermopylae to him by secret agreement. Philip now crushed Phocis, broke it up into small villages and took its seats on the Amphictyonic Council.

Most Greek states, Sparta excepted, then signed the Peace of Philocrates of 346BC, which recognized Philip's actions. The Sacred War was finally over. The real victor was neither Thebes nor Phocis but Macedonia, rising fast under its dynamic and cunning king to become the new hegemon of Greece.

MERCENARIES

The word 'mercenary' is pejorative today, but the Greeks called such soldiers either *xenoi* (foreigners) or, more politely, *epikuroi* (helpers). The profession, if scarcely glamorous, was not shameful. Greek mercenaries had fought in Egypt in the 6th century BC, and in the 5th century mercenary *peltasts* (light troops) were used at times. But only in the aftermath of the long Peloponnesian War (431–404BC) did mercenaries become important. Greeks who knew no other trade than soldiering now sought employment as mercenaries. Arcadia, the impoverished heart of the Peloponnese, was a major source of such soldiers, but they came from other cities facing hard times too. Probably the most famous was Xenophon. An Athenian ill at ease with his city's restored democracy, Xenophon, joined the army of the rebel Prince Cyrus in 401BC. He ended leading the '10,000', the Greek hoplites forming the army's core, back to the Greek world. He was not the only such mercenary, however.

Conon, the one Athenian *strategos* to escape the disaster at Aegospotamae in 405BC, hired himself out to the Persians over the next years, fighting Sparta at sea. Other 4th-century Athenian generals at times fought as mercenaries when they could not pay their armies, among them Iphicrates and Timotheus, two of Athens' best generals. More remarkably, King Agesilaus of Sparta (ruled 399–360BC) in his last years took service in Egypt, in revolt against Persia, to earn money for his now desperately strained city. This did attract criticism, however, since Spartan kings were descendants of the divine hero Hercules, not just ordinary generals.

Demosthenes, Athens' great 4th-century orator, often chided his fellow citizens for relying on mercenaries rather than fighting themselves. But in real emergencies Athenian citizens would still fight, as they did at Chaeronea in 338BC (if unsuccessfully). Since many wars in the 4th century hardly seemed worth fighting, hiring skilled mercenaries often seemed preferable.

Above: The tomb of Dioscorides, a mercenary. Mercenaries became common in Greek armies from the 4th century BC onwards, as ordinary citizens grew less inclined to fight.

MACEDONIA'S RISE TO POWER
359–336 BC

North of Mt Olympus, mythical home of the gods, lay Macedonia – to other Greeks a huge, strange, half-barbaric country. It had played an often ambiguous role in Greek affairs since the reign of Alexander I, king during the Persian invasion of 480BC. Although Macedonia had had ambitious monarchs, its frequent relapses into chaos meant that it was never more than a local power. All this changed with astonishing swiftness, however, when Philip II came to the throne in 359BC.

PHILIP'S POLICY OF EXPANSION
Philip had spent his youth as a hostage in Thebes, where he admired the military skills that gave Thebes its brief hegemony. Inheriting the Macedonian throne after his brother Perdiccas III was killed fighting Illyrian tribes, he defeated the invaders decisively in 358BC, pushing inland as far as Lake Ochrid. In 357BC Philip married the Epirote princess Olympias, who bore him a son, Alexander, in 356BC. That same year he seized Amphipolis, the key city founded by Athens but lost in 424BC, which

Above: Philip II, the ruler who transformed Macedonia from chaotic backwater to Greek superpower, was only 24 when he came to the throne in 359BC.

Above: The lion commemorating the Sacred Band, the elite corps of 300 Thebans killed at the Battle of Chaeronea in 338BC.

Below: At Chaeronea, Philip on the right feigned retreat, drawing on the Athenians, who exposed their flank to a cavalry charge by Alexander.

controlled the crossing of the River Strymon. Philip conned the Athenians into thinking that he was taking it for them, but kept it himself. With Amphipolis came the gold mines of Mt Pangaeus. Philip exploited these far more energetically, its gold underpinning his growing strength. He reorganized the Macedonian army, no longer basing regiments on clans or families. He created the Macedonian phalanx, a porcupine of pikesmen, and formed the Companions, a royal guard of elite cavalry. With this new,

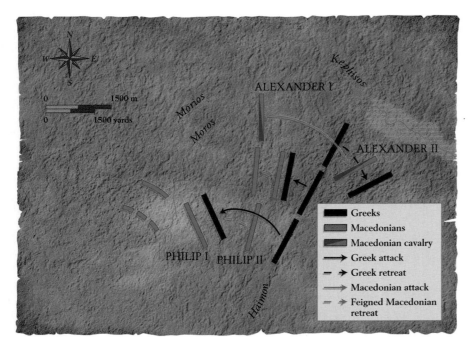

▮	Greeks
▮	Macedonians
▮	Macedonian cavalry
→	Greek attack
⇢	Greek retreat
→	Macedonian attack
⇢	Feigned Macedonian retreat

increasingly professional army under his excellent general Parmenion, he began his policy of relentless expansion.

In 356BC Philip took Pydna and Potidaea, cities on Macedonia's own coast, and captured Crenides inland on the Thracian border. Defeated in Thessaly by Phocis' superior numbers in 353BC, he took revenge soon after at the Battle of the Crocus Field, routing the Phocians with his cavalry. This victory made Philip *tagus* of Thessaly, controlling the port of Pagasae, and he added Thessaly's superb cavalry to his army.

A THREAT TO ATHENS

Although Philip was checked at Thermopylae in 352BC by Athens, he had transformed Macedonia's position. He could do this because the southern Greeks were distracted by other events: Thebes by the Sacred War; Athens by the revolt of its allies and Mausolus of Caria; and Sparta by problems close to home. In 349BC Philip besieged Olynthus, the main Chalcidic city. The Athenians, despite an alliance with it, did nothing to help and

Below: Demosthenes, Athens' last great democrat and a renowned orator, whose Philippics *(speeches against Philip) led his city finally to fight Macedonia.*

Philip captured it in 348BC, razing it to the ground. In 347BC Philip turned east to conquer the area around the River Hebrus in Thrace. His growing power now started to threaten Athens' vital grain supplies through the Hellespont.

When Thebes asked Philip for help against Phocis in 346BC, he marched south, finding Thermopylae unguarded. He trounced the Phocians, whom he denounced for stealing Apollo's gold, taking their seats on the Amphictyonic Council (a great coup, for it meant Macedonia's recognition as fully Greek), and presided over the Pythian games. The war-weary Greeks accepted his new status in the Peace of Philocrates. But he had grander plans: to be hegemon of Greece.

BATTLE OF CHAERONEA

In 342BC Philip marched north-east into wild Thrace. Despite falling gravely ill, he made all Thrace acknowledge his suzerainty. Alarmed at developments, which further threatened Athens' Black Sea grain, Demosthenes persuaded Perinthus and Byzantium to turn against Philip. In 339BC, when Philip besieged Byzantium, Athens declared war and sent a fleet, forcing him to withdraw. Philip, seizing 200 grain ships meant for Athens, marched into Phocis.

Demosthenes now persuaded Athens to offer an alliance to Thebes, its old rival. A tense debate in Thebes led to acceptance. The two great powers of old Greece (Sparta being now insignificant) mobilized. The two armies met at Chaeronea in August 338BC. Philip's right wing, facing the inexperienced Athenians, feigned a retreat. As the Athenians advanced, they opened a gap between themselves and the Thebans into which Prince Alexander charged with the Macedonian cavalry. Then Philip's disciplined troops turned to counter-attack. The Athenians fled. Only the Theban Sacred Band stood its ground to the last man. The Battle of Chaeronea had proved fatal to Greek liberty.

Above: A coin showing Dionysus, god of wine and ecstasy, widely worshipped in Macedonia and Thrace.

Below: This fine bronze statue of a youth, made c.340BC and found in the sea, suggests that by the mid-4th century BC Greeks lacked their earlier heroic determination.

THE END OF CLASSICAL GREECE 337–322BC

Above: Lycurgus of Athens, in control of the city's finances for 12 years, oversaw the construction of new shipyards and the rebuilding of the Theatre of Dionysus.

Below: In 338BC Philip called a Panhellenic Congress at Corinth, chosen because it had been the seat of resistance during the Persian Wars.

Philip used his crushing victory at Chaeronea wisely, as might be expected from such an astutely diplomatic leader. He treated Thebes, which had broken its treaty with Macedonia, more severely than Athens, placing a Macedonian garrison in the Cadmaea (the citadel of Thebes) but giving Athens the border town of Oropus. Philip himself returned 2,000 Athenian captives, but retained the Chersonese peninsula so that he could cut Athens' grain supplies at will. Philip then invaded the Peloponnese. Meeting no resistance, he ravaged Spartan territory, leaving it yet more isolated and powerless but still feared by its neighbours.

In 338–337BC Philip established the League of Corinth to promulgate his grand design: a Panhellenic war against Persia to avenge its attack on Greece nearly 150 years earlier. For this he ideally wanted Athenian naval help and certainly a quiescent Greece behind him. To ensure the latter, he planted Macedonian garrisons at Ambracia in the west, Chalcis on Euboea and Corinth. The Greeks voted him Captain General of the Greeks and he sent an advance force into Asia. But he himself never followed it. Returning to Macedonia, he celebrated the marriage of his daughter with her uncle Alexander of Cleopatra (he had already divorced Olympias, Alexander's mother). When in 336BC Philip was assassinated, seemingly for personal reasons, many in Greece must have expected Macedonia to relapse into its customary chaos. They were to be devastatingly disappointed.

ALEXANDER AND GREECE

Rapidly establishing himself as Philip's heir, the 20-year-old Alexander raced down into Greece – cutting steps in the sides of Mt Ossa when the Thessalians demurred at letting him pass – to squash potential revolts. Thessaly accepted him as its leader and the League at Corinth elected him General. Returning north, he swept through Thrace, crossing the Danube – the first Greek soldier to do so – before turning west to defeat the Illyrians. There he heard that the Thebans, believing a rumour of his death, had risen and massacred some Macedonian officers, besieging the rest of the garrison in the citadel. Returning south at lightning speed, he stormed Thebes in September 335BC, razing the ancient city to the ground and enslaving its inhabitants.

After this act of exemplary terror, Greece was cowed. Alexander took only 20 ships from Athens when he crossed into Asia in 334BC, mainly as hostages. He left Antipater, one of his best generals, with an army in Macedonia to control Greece. Many Greeks secretly hoped for

ATHENS REBUILDS ITSELF

During the peaceful if drought-stricken years of Alexander's conquest of Asia, Athens enjoyed an autumnal calm. She rebuilt her dockyards, increasing her fleet to 400 galleys. Lycurgus, effectively Finance Minister for 12 years from 338BC, reconstructed the city's theatre of Dionysus, built the Panathenaic Stadium and rebuilt the Lyceum. There the philosopher Aristotle used to take his walks, teaching as he went, giving the name 'Peripatetic' (from *peripatetikos*, to pace to and fro) to his school. The Laurium silver mines were reopened, and the military training of *ephebi* (young citizens aged 18–20) was reorganized.

Alexander's defeat and death. In 331BC, Agis III of Sparta, a young monarch with more ambition than sense but financed by Persian gold, rose against the Macedonians. His army was routed at Megalopolis by Antipater and he was killed. Greece lapsed into acquiescence.

THE EXILES' DECREE

In 324BC Alexander issued an edict ordering every Greek city to take back its exiles. This caused problems for some cities, especially Athens. Its *cleruchs* had colonized Samos, so Samian exiles wanted their land back. Athens sent envoys to remonstrate with Alexander. (His other demand – that he be worshipped as a god – caused relatively few problems, for some Greeks had already been given divine honours.) Meanwhile Harpalus, a corrupt Macedonian high official, appeared at Athens with quantities of gold, some of which Demosthenes allegedly took. Then came the long-awaited news: Alexander was dead.

THE LAMIAN WAR

At first few could believe it. "If he were dead, the whole world would stink of his corpse!" declared Demades, an orator.

But as the Greeks realized that it was true, many joined Athens' revolt against the Macedonians. (Aristotle, tainted by his associations – he had been Alexander's tutor – fled from Athens to avoid it "repeating its mistake with Socrates".)

The Athenians seized Thermopylae and kept Antipater and his army beseiged in the city of Lamia through the winter of 323–322BC. But despite this initial success, the Lamian War went badly for the allied Greeks: they often did not agree on their actions, their best general, Leosthenes, was killed in the siege and Athens could not afford to man more than half of its new fleet.

After reinforcements reached Antipater from Asia, he broke out. At the Battle of Crannon in August 322BC the combined Macedonians defeated the Greeks decisively. This time peace was truly dictated. Athens' democracy became an oligarchy, with a Macedonian garrison in the Piraeus. The democratic leaders fled into exile, Demosthenes taking poison rather than face capture. With him died classical Greece.

Above: Philip in later life, arbiter of Greece, supremely experienced both as a general and a diplomat.

Below: The plains of Boeotia, called the 'dance floor of Ares (Mars)' because many battles were fought there. Alexander, by destroying Thebes in 335BC, shocked Greece into accepting his power.

INDEX